I Am My Sister's Keeper

Compiled by *Telishia Berry*

Publisher & Editor-in-Chief of
Courageous Woman Magazine

ISBN-13: 978-0-9786001-6-7

Strive Publishing is a division of Courageous Media Group. For more information on the authors, ordering, book signings, or to sponsor an event, contact us at: info@courageouswomanmag.com.

Edited/formatted by Shonell Bacon

Dedication

This book is dedicated to every sister's keeper out there. May you also have sister's keepers to watch over and help you on your journey.

Foreword

To be asked to write a foreword for a book about women who exhibit love and empathy through their strength and support of other women is an absolute honor. For me, Telishia Berry is that kind of woman. I met her over 10 years ago when she contacted me regarding a feature interview about my women's empowerment practice for her publication, *Courageous Woman Magazine*, which she was launching at the time. We began to talk as scheduled for the interview and instantly had a connection. Amazingly, what was supposed to be a half-hour interview turned into several hours of sister sharing, bonding, and encouragement. We have been friends ever since.

Telishia is a person with a huge heart, and she has love for everyone in her circle and for those who are connected to those she loves. She is my friend, and a particularly good one, I might add, and I pride myself in sharing a loving sister's keeper relationship with her for more than a decade. It is a friendship that has taken us through our share of debates as well as our share of opportunities, encouragement, and support.

As an emotional intelligence practitioner that empowers women to live their dreams, I work with women who feel they have no one to personally share their trials and triumphs. Many felt alone in their pain and were afraid to seek advice from other women because of their own feelings of shame and the fear of rejection and judgment. As their coach, I play an intricate role as a surrogate sister's keeper in guiding these women through doubt and disbelief into the confidence of living in their personal power.

As women, we are natural nurturers, and we have the propensity to be empathic and quickly pick up the energetic signatures of other women. Sadly, many women are still captive to their own pain and quickly indulge in competitive socialized behavior that pits us against each other rather than allowing us to come together as siStars in love and community. In this book, Telishia offers us a glimpse into the workings of the sister's keeper relationship that cultivates community and our growth as women through the cumulative real-life stories of the women featured in this text.

Kudos to my friend Telishia Berry for compiling and publishing the stories of the following women who have contributed to the making of this book. It is a testament to the power of sisterhood and how the love of our commonalities as women bond us together as we continue to encourage and support each other. This book also inspires us to continue sisterly traditions by investing our time in each other as a sister's keeper to promote our strengths, both collectively and individually, because we are most assuredly stronger together.

Ladies, we are not an island, and there is no need to suffer through when we have siStars in our corner that are willing to give of their open hearts and wisdom. Their love for us lends us the shoulder we need to cry on while providing us with a firm push that keeps us moving forward.

I am humbled by the opportunity to share with you, the reader, the power that is showcased in this book by the contributing women who have openly shared intimate stories of their personal trials and triumphs that have brought about their own transformations through the grace and love of the women in their own lives.

Oh, so what happened to my interview with Telishia? Well, amusingly it would be some eight years later before we revisited the interview for her magazine. However, by that time, her business had grown, and she then wanted to interview me for her radio show of the same title. We laughed and joked back then, wondering if we could get beyond our siStar chats to make it happen. We chose to turn that conversation into the radio interview.

Dr. Diva Verdun, PhD

Creator of the Feminine Manifestation Model

Contents

Acknowledgments

Thank you to my four reflections that inspire me to keep going: Kendre', Tisha, Toi, and Kennedy.

I also acknowledge and give thanks to editor Shon Bacon for her expertise and work on our books and to Editorial Manager Dr. Ladel Lewis for her tireless contributions.

I want to give a great big hug and thank you to the many Sister Keepers that played a major role in my life at the most critical times in my life—Apostle Sandra Appleberry, Apostle Tiffany Baker, and Dr. Diva Verdun.

What Is a Sister's Keeper?

A Sister's Keeper, to me, is someone who is spiritually appointed and assigned to you. She is someone who has an open heart and a listening ear without judgment. She is a friend who gives good counsel, consoles, and offers you a box of tissues or chocolates if you need them. A Sister's Keeper simply tells it like it is and doesn't hesitate to provide constructive criticism or get you "told"—with love in a sisterly way. She keeps your deepest secrets and lends you her shoulder when you need to cry. A Sister's Keeper encourages, uplifts, and empowers her sisters. She will have your back when you least expect it. She doesn't hold any punches or bite her tongue to tell you the truth. She ministers and prays for you and leads you with spiritual guidance. She will make you laugh when you can't find anything to laugh about. Most of all, she will remind you of who you are and the person God called you to be.

While going through one of the darkest seasons in my life, the breakup of my marriage, I prayed a lot. I cried out to God for HELP because of the emotional and verbal abuse I was suffering. He sent me help in the form of women of God. They were counselors, ministers, and women of wisdom. At first, I didn't understand who they were. I didn't know the women.

I Am My Sister's Keeper

I would meet them in grocery stores, restaurants, churches. We somehow connected and became friends, or they would ask if they could pray for me. One of them was my former pastor's wife. She said she could see the frown behind my smile and that I was very weary. She was right. She said she was waiting for me to talk with her, but I wasn't ready to talk at that time. During a visit to another church, the pastor called me out for prayer. She put her hand on my heart and said she could feel my pain. More women from the congregation surrounded me in prayer. There were many women whom I met during that season that prayed for me, counseled me, and encouraged me. They pushed me to not only share my testimony but to use my platform to help other women. When I think of them, I imagine them like soldiers. They came to rescue me. I realized they were the answer to my prayers. I called them my Sister's Keepers.

I wanted to publish this book in honor of the many Sister's Keepers who have been there for me during the most pivotal times in my life. And for those of you who couldn't put a name or title to the "Show up" sisters who were present in your lives. They are your Sister's Keepers.

I Am My Sister's Keeper

I have a great deal of love and respect for the Sister's Keepers who played major roles in my life's journey. I am where I am today because of the many Sister Keepers in my life.

The contributing authors included in this book share their most personal and inspiring stories of hope, restoration, and change. I know you will be enlightened and encouraged by these amazing stories and testimonies.

Beautiful Scars

Lisa Allgood

How can a scar be beautiful?

When I was a kid, I was a tomboy. I ran around climbing trees and jumping off roofs of abandoned houses. I would get all kinds of cuts and bruises, and when the cuts healed, I would pull the dead skin off and smile, looking at that ugly scar and thinking, wow the beautiful lessons I learned from getting those scars, but those were scars on my 6-year-old body. I had much bigger scars on the inside that I did not know how to fix as a child. I had trust and abandonment issues, which are far too heavy for a child to carry around. Add to that the feeling that you are alone, worthless, and unloved.

A scar reminds you that there was hurt, there was pain, there was a wound but not anymore. The body has completely repaired itself. When we think about healing, we often only think about the body. But what about your heart and mind? We don't give the care and attention to wounds on our hearts and minds. For years, we walk around, wounded, not getting the proper help to heal those wounds. How do you heal social, mental, or spiritual wounds?

It has been said that time heals all wounds. I don't agree. The wounds remain. Time - the mind, protecting its sanity - covers them with some scar tissue and the pain lessens, but it is never gone. -Rose Kennedy

In the healing process, I find that time is particularly important. You can't rush it. I tried to rush it, and it only made me hurt more. I found myself mad at the world and everyone around me. My hurt and pain caused me not to trust anyone. It made me feel like no one loved me. Or I wasn't good enough. I could not trust a soul. I always thought everyone was out to get me. That is, until one day when a good friend told me I needed to forgive myself. I know what you are probably thinking: girl, what did you need to forgive yourself for? Trust me, it will all make sense.

I Am My Sister's Keeper

Dear 6-year-old Lisa, it is not your fault that someone abused you. Someone was supposed to protect you. Not everybody in this world wants to hurt you.

Dear 13-year-old Lisa, you are beautiful. So what, the other kids don't see it. Every day, you need to wake up, look in the mirror, and say, "I am beautiful."

Dear 17-year-old Lisa, the moment you cut your wrist, you felt unloved, and you felt like life wasn't worth living. The pain got too hard to carry.

Dear 37-year-old Lisa, I forgive you. For years, you have walked around hurt and in pain. Not anymore. You must heal. It is time. We carry unhealed and infected wounds around our whole entire life. While sitting in church one Sunday morning, I heard the preacher say loud and clear:

You can't walk in faith and fear at the same time. -Brenad Johnson

Dear 40-year-old Lisa, it feels awesome to wake up every morning with a free spirit. You are not weighed down by all the hurt and pain from your past. You walk through your day with not one worry. That feeling of fear is a thing of the past. You are taking more chances, living every day with a smile on your face no matter what may happen in that day. I love you, girl. I love your smile; it's bright and welcoming. The world could be crashing down all around us, but your smile will just make everything seem all right. I like your personality; you're quiet in a sense, but you can be loud when you need to be. I love when you show the funny side of you. You seem to be free when you're just letting go. You should do that more. I love your heart; it has always been big and caring. I like that you give your heart freely. Even through hurt and pain, your heart stays big. I like your eyes; when I look into them, I see expectation like you're waiting for something to happen. There is hope in your eyes, a forever hope like you will never give up until you see it type of hope. I love your passion for perfection. You know that you can't be perfect or make the world perfect, but when you make the littlest things perfect, the whole world seems better. I love you. You're beautiful inside and out, you are an amazing person, and the world needs to know you.

Stop hiding behind all the hurt and pain that others have caused you. You're an awesome woman, full of light and love. Ms. Allgood, it is all good. Your name is great and so are you. Stop hiding, stop making yourself small. It won't work. Every time you walk in a room, the atmosphere changes because you bring greatness with you. If you haven't noticed, it draws people to you. Open your mind and heart, it's ok. You have something to give this world, so stop holding back. Girl, your name is being mentioned in rooms you haven't even stepped in yet. Be Great!

Sincerely, Lisa M. Allgood

You can heal. Now, I won't lie to you; it's going to be hard. But it will be worth it. Just think about how free you will be. Start journaling and getting your thoughts out on paper. Stop holding things in. Call a good friend that's going to keep it 100% real with you and talk to them. Most importantly, pray, seek God for the healing that you need. He *will* give it to you. Remember, he cares for you. And he loves you. By the end of your healing process, you will have beautiful scars.

■ · ■ · ■ · ■ · ■ · ■ · ■ · ■ · ■ · ■ · ■ · ■ · ■ · ■ · ■ · ■

Lisa Michelle Allgood is a small-town girl with a big heart. There is nothing that she would not do to make sure a person is taken care of. Lisa relays on her faith to get her through rough times. She became a minister on December 31, 2018. Becoming a leader in her community is her next, and biggest goal. Changing the lives of others is what she strives to do every day by encouraging them with words, or just a simple smile. She is a mother, daughter, sister, and a best friend.

Healing of My Heart

Stacey Bulluck

Have you ever asked yourself, why did I do that? I know, unfortunately, this question is only asked after a life event has taken place, it's over, and now we have the 20/20 hindsight vision. We can feel and see the effects. In my instance, it was what I felt—more accurately, what I did not feel. I was numb, desensitized, deadened to everything: love, family, friendship. You name it, I was numb to it. Good, bad—it did not matter.

My life could have been described using the first stanza of Sade's song "Soldier of Love." The lyrics are, "I've lost the use of my heart, but I'm still alive." My heart had been snuffed out, and I felt helpless and depleted. At that time, I didn't have the ability to think, feel, do, or be. My heart did not move me to fulfill my purpose. I was stuck. Deprived of the power of sensation. No feeling, senseless. All I had was an emotional tornado in my life, and it was taking precedence over everything regarding my heart and mind. My emotions were unresponsive, paralyzed. I had existed in a loveless, disrespectful, mentally abusive marriage for a decade. I had to abruptly get out of the military in 2002 after almost 18 years of service because of an injury I sustained while serving in Sinai, Egypt, in 1997. Was it not bad enough that while on my last duty assignment I suffered major financial losses? At that time, I was married, and we moved from Washington, DC, to El Paso, Texas, because the military said so. This warranted that my husband leave his union job, and I had to stop being a part-time real estate agent. NO, it didn't stop there, my military pay was reduced by $2,000 monthly. We went from bringing home $5,000 to $8,000 monthly to bringing home $2,000 monthly. Guess what? We still had our same expenses with the addition of rent for our home in El Paso. Life tried to shoot its best shot. Although I lost a lot of tangible things, they were not as important as the feeling I had during these trying times: I was being strengthened for the greatest demonstration of a life that is resilient and strong.

Life will bring its stuff, but now I am living every day making the choice to be cognizant in the process of preparation for the great things to come, and when the tornadic winds blow, I will not get destroyed.

We need tools for building a permanent plan to fulfill purpose and get a clear understanding about what it will take to walk in freedom to be prolific human beings. I had to get out of the "without form and void" state and, to instead, discover and learn, how to BE in the intended state of manifesting my God-given purpose on earth, which is being a living soul and thriving from the place where life was originally infused. We must be determined. As Maya Angelou said, "I can be changed by what happens to me but I refuse to be reduced by it." We will not allow anything to stop or deteriorate our purpose, nor will our view of who we are be reduced in our own mind where we begin to believe the negative mantra that says we will not overcome life's challenges. Let's get a firm grip on what is growing and developing in our hearts and minds. Our hearts are the breeding ground for the life of abundance and vitality.

Keep your heart with all diligence, For out of it spring the issues of life. -Proverbs 4:23

As diligent as I was toward staying in a relationship that did not serve me, it was imperative I became two times more committed to preserving my place of peace and areas of life that had been degraded with emotional abuse and pain. Because my heart was broken into pieces nothing was able to spring forth or come out. No purpose or passion, it was deteriorated. Adjustments were needed in my behavior. I was demonstrating that I had no hope. Therefore, I kept giving in to the debilitated state of mind. I had dipped down so low my actions showed as if I were someone with a brain injury. This brings my mind to a verse that says, "we are to keep our hearts with all diligence, because this is the source of where our life stems from." The place where we have our behavioral motivations. A psychologist named Abraham Maslow used the terms "physiological," "safety," "belonging and love," "social needs" or "esteem," and "self-actualization" to describe the areas where human beings need fulfillment in order to access this place where life flows. His theory is one area cannot be fulfilled if the other is not. Meaning if we do not have our basic needs of food, water, safe shelter, love, and the feeling of belonging, it may be difficult for an individual to have high self-esteem. Now, they are not motivated to produce behaviors that are fundamentally sound and give them the backbone to stand up and conquer issues while on this journey. We must guard all areas of life. We want to show up to the world as strong, confident, and purpose driven women.

I Am My Sister's Keeper

The human spirit is strongest when it's focused and moving in purpose. I learned when I am persistent and diligent in my pursuit of who I am there is no stopping me. When we have our attention centered on our dreams, passions, hopes, and desires, this demonstrates the heart has been divinely healed, inspirationally, and cohesively flowing in creativity and producing the desires of your heart. It functions to the highest capacity in its most intensive frame of mind. This frame of mind or way of thinking renews the heart, and now we function in the being part of why we were created. We were created to change the society we live in. It is the most awesome feeling when you come to this realization. Coming into the knowledge of who we are and why we are helps in the process of bringing into captivity thoughts and imaginations that could lead us in the opposite direction of our God-given purpose.

The way we accomplish our God given purpose is by being sure to carefully examine what is being kept in your heart because everything we do flows from the heart. Nothing should impede the flow or stop your growth and purpose development. It is necessary to always guard your heart from allowing negative destroying words to get stored there. We will achieve this by having a diligent lifestyle. Being meticulous about what and who we allow to come in. We can set our mind on the things that show God's goodness in the earth. Because, after all, as a spiritual being, it is God's Spirit exhaling into us the gale force winds of change in our lives, so we have what it takes to help others change their lives. God is skillfully blowing his energy deep within you, eagerly working in you what to will and to do. This is what gives Him the most pleasure. Preparing and improving you for the expansion of his greatness in you.

Remember though, with greatness comes responsibility, and I want us to be prepared. No longer will pain, hurt, rejection, or disappointment catch us off guard. Our lives are not like a country that is not adequately equipped when a pandemic crisis arrives. Scrambling in chaos. We are healed and whole, armed with tools of high self-esteem and confidence. Now, we are well on our way of getting to the top of Maslow's hierarchy of needs. Nothing missing, broken, or lacking. Totally taking life on, and having more energy and determination, which produce better relationships and the feeling we are connected. Our confidence is showing up to the world around us and generating influence as well as growing in our emotional state; now we behave more responsibly. It's great to feel whole. Physically, spiritually, and emotionally we are in bounce back mode.

This to me, my friend, is as important as breathing; you have the capacity to recover (improve) quickly from difficulties. That just means you are resilient, and yes, you are. You have come a long way further than you know. Just from the beginning of the chapter up to this point, you have the capacity to embrace difficulty, and it does not consume who you are. You should get excited here! We are no longer enslaved to heartache or difficult life challenges. No, we're not exempt, but it has no power. Say it out loud, heartache has no power! At this very moment, we are balanced and steady, having great expectations of moving forward. We have our awareness, consciousness back, if you will. Our spiritual and mental senses are effectively working. Harvard says resilience has many health benefits, such as "longevity and greater satisfaction with life."

So know that you *are* resilient!

————————————————————————

Stacey Bulluck is an author and transformational speaker, committed to igniting resilience and building life skills of her clients and audiences. Through her messages of inspiration, motivation, and transformation individuals regain power to become emotionally healed and capable of persevering through opposition, making us stronger and better equipped to fulfill purpose.

Stacey is the author of two books, *Beaten Oil* and *Regain Power Through Resilience: Don't Let Your Brain Go Numb.* These manuscripts impart lessons which explain how readers utilize their inner light as a guide for others and how to rediscover strength to bounce back when life is challenging.

Master the Art of Forgiveness

Angela Clifton

You shall be a crown of beauty in the hand of the Lord, and a royal diadem in the hand of your God. You shall no more be termed Forsaken, and your land shall no more be termed Desolate; but you shall be called My Delight Is in Her... for the Lord delights in you...—Isaiah 62:3-4 NRSV

"The world needs
Strong women.
 Women who will
lift and *build others*,
 who will
love and *be loved*.
 Women who
live bravely, both
tender and *fierce*.
 Women of
indomitable will." –Amy Tenney

Have you ever heard someone say that forgiveness is not for you; it's for others who have hurt you? Forgiveness Will Make You Free...

I admit forgiving others wasn't something I was good at, and for so many years, I was horrible at it with good reason and justification; unforgiveness has a long...memory, and it will eventually rob you of your life's peace, health, love, joy, and so much more.

I battled with issues of forgiving others, and as a result, I suffered loneliness, depression, anxiety, stress, low self-esteem, and constant worry. I was very depressed and had trust issues. There was a lot going on inside of me that led to poor decision making, unhealthy thinking, and wrong relationships. Holding on to unforgiveness caused me to hold grudges against people for the smallest things. You see, it didn't come out of thin air. I dealt with sexual abuse at age 5, and from there on, I suffered with many problems in my life. Demons and nightmares that I couldn't shake. God is good though; he delivered me of my past of sexual abuse. He set me free, but it was a process. God will take your ashes and replace them with beauty and blessings beyond what you have prayed for.

He'll give you glory for your story. Sister, there is purpose in your pain. God will turn it around for you, but you have got to let go of whatever it is that's keeping you bound. Weeping may endure for a night, but joy is coming in the morning. There is hope on the other side of the mountain. Many seasons, I had to go through the process to receive my healing, deliverance, and breakthroughs in order to get to the place God was taking me and the place I am today.

The work had to be done. I was willing because I knew that there was something more to my life. I put my focus on positive things, and I surrounded myself with positive people. However, I do believe that there's a strong chance that things could have changed a lot sooner in my life if I would have surrendered early on. I believe that holding on to the hurt, pain, and bitterness of the unforgiveness in my heart caused me to stay in the wilderness a little longer.

I wasn't ready to let go of the past. I had grew accustomed to the dysfunction in my life. I was comfortable, and it became my normal. I thought everyone else was the problem. I couldn't see my wrongs, my faults. I couldn't see that I was inflicting my pain upon others. I was hurt and broken; for so long, in my mind, I was fine. There was nothing wrong with me.

Everyone's preparation season is different. It may even look different, but however God decides to bring you out, count it all joy. Woman of God, you will get there, and you will win. Whatever you have gone through, whatever you may be facing today or experiencing, Jesus has already given you the grace to come out of it safe and unharmed. There'll be no smoke or residue on you. People won't believe it's you. Trust the process; you are victorious and more than a conqueror. You can overcome any and everything that God has allowed you go through. God is preparing you for something greater. Your setbacks are just setups. God is setting you up to win souls and so much more. I salute you, sis, because you are the real MVP in the Kingdom of God. You have an inheritance of opulent opportunities, riches, health, wealth, success, and love—so much is waiting on you.

For I know the plans I have for you,
declares the LORD, plans to prosper you
and not to harm you, plans to give you
hope and a future –Jeremiah 29:11

SHE IS clothed
with STRENGTH
& DIGNITY
and laughs
WITHOUT Fear
of the FUTURE –Proverbs 31:25

21

I Am My Sister's Keeper

In 2016, I took a long sabbatical. It was in that time that I received my healing finally. I say finally because I had to learn that everything we need is already done and waiting on us. Jesus took care of everything for us; he made sure that you and I were good before he went to be with the Father. I was so ready to let go of my dark past and move forward with my life. I was in a space where I was truly ready to receive God's peace and harmony, serenity, and healing. And for the very first time in my life, I was UNAPOLOGETIC and brave about it, ready to take my life back...and my power. I wanted to be set FREE, for whom the Son sets free is free indeed.

Since then, I have been moving forward, looking straight ahead, enjoying my new journey, and making preparation for what's next because greater is coming, and I'm extremely excited, grateful, hopeful, and optimistic about what's ahead for me. I know my future is bright and so is yours! Surround yourself with people of influence. Instrumental people pray for right connections; it is so important who you connect with because wrong people will be an obstacle for you.

During my sabbatical, I discovered a lot about myself, things I love about me and even some things I disliked. It is so important to do the work; nothing happens until you make a move. There were things I wanted to improve, so I focused a lot on generosity, kindness, and positivity. I wanted to make better choices. Do new things. I wanted to travel the world and meet new people and experience more in life. Indulge in foods I'd never tasted before. I'm the kind of girl who'll eat cupcakes and birthday cake just because. I find reasons to celebrate myself. I find reasons to be happy. I love having *girlfriend time*, being childlike at heart, and putting all of my focus and energy on creating an extraordinary life. There is a whole list of wonderful things I dream of seeing myself doing and having. Manifestation starts in the mind.

I would love to be more adventurous. I focused on marriage, femininity, business, family, and also on health, well-being, and entrepreneurship. My life was changing, and I realized during that time how much I need God for everything concerning my life. I began to pour out to God about how much I wanted to teach women how beautiful and powerful it is to operate in their femininity. I watched a lot of the old classical movies, studying women learning things about how to be a class act lady: poised, classy, elegant, and sophisticated, smart, intelligent, and respectful.

I shared so many of dreams and desires with the Lord, and I knew he was listening and taking notes. I was ready to receive all of his best, to be in his perfect divine will. I felt safe and secure with God like never before. I became bolder and more confident. My self-esteem increased and so did my value. I was hungry and thirsty, and the more God spoke to my spirit and showed me things in the spirit, the more I was becoming Christ like. I thought about how much I wanted to help women achieve success and how to help them understand their self-worth. I wanted to help build women from the inside outside. I love to encourage my sisters around the world, cheer them on, and celebrate them. I want to see generations change and generational curses lifted off family blood lines.

I am so very appreciative of the Lord's goodness in my life. Being in his presence is beautiful. I experience this warm, fuzzy, cozy feeling. God's love, care, and concern for us is so beautiful. The more you spend time alone in his presence, the more you grow supreme confidence in him.

God's laughter is contagious! Sometimes, I find myself laughing so hard deep within. He is joyful, exciting, and has the best sense of humor. Experiencing his exuberant love is amazing. It's awesome and incredible to know him this way and how he radiates a type of energy unexplainable.

You will encounter a space in him that's full of love, hope, zest, and zing. He is zealous and compassionate toward us. He's kind, so thoughtful, generous, and loving. My relationship with the Lord is growing and so am I. If you're not careful, you'll fall in heavenly love with him in such a way that you'll think he's magical.

I feel good about my transformation, what is taking place inside and outside of me. I never want to give that up. You will know what real love feels like before the mate comes, and you won't except nothing less. You'll begin to experience the exuberance of God's love in everything you do.

Sister Girl, EXUBERANT JOY is resting upon you for miraculous change and unusual favor. You are kind, so beautiful and smart. You have so much to offer, so much to give, and so much to teach others. You are a woman who overflows in grace, abundance, love, and true beauty. You know your identity; you know who you are and whose you are.

Say it out loud: I AM PHENOMENAL! Phenomenal woman, you are worthy to be praised. God made you in his likeness…his image. You have the wisdom of Solomon 2:23.

Do you know that you are wanted, needed? Sister Girl, you are necessary for such a time as this. Women all over the world are waiting on you to bust a move. They need what you have inside of you to be deposited inside of them. I pray that we as woman will get back to God's original plan, even in our femininity because that is where our true power, beauty, essence, and sexiness is. It's in our womanhood. God is counting on us; he's calling your name.

Sister, he needs your brilliance, intelligence, your extraordinary expertise in every area. Let's get back to God's original plan, even concerning men. When we get back in order, so too will families in future generations.

The men in our lives need us. Our husbands, sons, sons-in-law, fathers, and grandfathers.

Your family and friends, they need you also. It's your season. Your time to shine like the diamond you are.

I came to push you, elevate your conscious mind, remind you that you matter even when you don't see it. You have everything you need, and you are suited and booted up for what God has assigned to your life.

Change your attitude, and you will change your life. You are God's exuberant love demonstrated in the earth. You are a chosen vessel, and God wants to use you to help bring change to the earth, change in your family, the nation, and so much more. You have been faithful, and You are the woman for the job. God is a rewarder, and he's rewarding you with all of his best kingdom blessings. You are God's masterpiece.

God is rewarding you with 5 Crowns for your faithfulness:

1. The Crown of Life
2. Incorruptible Crown
3. Crown of Righteousness
4. Crown of Glory
5. Crown of Exultation

You are royalty, and your crowns represent:

- Power
- Legitimacy
- Triumph
- Honor
- Glory
- Immortality
- Righteousness
- Resurrection

Remember to remain humble and steadfast and to use your gifts wisely. Take nothing or no one for granted. Everything that comes from God is a gift. This is the day that the Lord has made; rejoice, be happy, thankful, glad, and grateful in it. Sister, remember this too shall pass. No matter what, trouble don't last always. There's so much to be thankful for. We are facing challenging times in the world and in the economy today like never before due to the COVID-19 Coronavirus. However, God is in control, and you are not in a Coronavirus crisis nor are you in a recession.

Take this time and use it well—even as a time of sabbatical and reflection. Consider how you can become better and do better with the precious life you have been gifted with and you are so very blessed to have.

Pray for our leaders, our president, our families, and friends. Pray for our neighbors, the people in our communities and around the world. Pray that the Lord's will be done. Pray about seen and unseen dangers, the things we may not know or hear. Fight the good fight of faith and have hope. Persevere during these tough, trying times, and put your full trust in our creator our Lord Savior Jesus Christ!

Lord, we trust the shift although we may not understand all the things going on today in the world and in our country. Lord, we trust you, and we believe that you will be on time. Lord, we cry out to you, ABBA Father, release healing in the land of the living. Father God, we declare healing in the world and in our homes and with our families. The hospitals, the jails, the schools, our jobs, and our businesses. The churches, Father God, and in our finances. God, we believe, and we know that you got the whole wide world in your hands. Hallelujah, Jesus Lord, what the world needs now is love, your forgiveness. We need you; we need your unconditional, exuberant love and protection to spread faster than this COVID-19 virus.

God, the world needs your grace and tender mercies, your guidance and instructions. We need your wisdom and strength. I pray Psalms 91's anointing of protection to rest upon every country and nation. Cover your people in the blood of Jesus almighty. Amen.

Life is constantly challenging us.
It provides us with
    frequent
opportunities to
overcome small
    hurdles.
As we learn to deal
with these hurdles, we
practice the strength
and resilience needed
to face the greater
obstacles ahead. –Suzy Lee

I Am My Sister's Keeper

Be encouraged and lifted up in your spirit. Take time to smell the roses. Not everything is about securing the bag. Practice gratitude, and master the art of forgiveness.

Take God as your partner. He is your source and soul provider.

Prophesy to your mountains. Speak blessings over your life. Practice having good energy and high vibrations, eat healthy, exercise, stay hydrated. Fast, detox, reduce stress and anxiety. Pray more, worry less. Be carefree, positive, and practice good habits. Start a new hobby, sing, dance, watch feel-good movies. Meditate on the word, read your bible, love your neighbors. Be good to your family and friends, spend quality time with the people you love, cherish them. Travel the world, try something new, do something new.

Make a list of the six most important things to do daily. Set a new goal, dream a bigger dream—live, laugh, love.

Best wishes and warm regards,

Angela Clifton

Angela Clifton is an inspiring entrepreneur and second-time author. In 2018, she wrote her very first book collaboration titled *The MizCEO Entrepreneurial Book Volume II: 20 Commandments for Women in Business*. She is also an independent beauty consultant for the amazing innovative powerhouse skincare company called MaryKay Cosmetics, which she absolutely enjoys very much. Angela is very passionate about helping women and loved being in alignment with amazing positive women who are likeminded in values. It is Angela's belief that everyone of us should strive to have a GO-GIVER spirit.

Website: www.marykay.com/aclifton17
Email: classey2angie@yahoo.com

The Letter from My Sister

Natasha Cooper

Have you ever found yourself smiling through the most difficult times in your life? Feeling the most pain! As if you don't know where your next step is coming from, not even your next breath.

However, you are the Sister/Friend that everyone else looks to so you don't let them down. You absorb all of their bumps and bruises, hurt and pain, and come up with the best solutions and advice in the world for everyone but yourself. You were there at the drop of a dime for everyone that calls, cries out, looks sad, needs guidance, needs a shoulder to cry on, a listening ear, or just to sit in silence and know you're there. FOR ANYTHING, for your children, for your family, for your job, you show up for everyone that needs you, but you never show up for you.

This was my life.

I feared letting people know that things were hard for me, that my life was not as it would appear to be, that I struggled with so many things including my marriage, the relationship between my son and my husband, my job, not doing what I thought I was supposed to be doing in life.

I had so many fears, but I had to continue to shine my light for others to see and stay in darkness alone because I could not let anyone see the dark days that I had because they needed me, or at least that's what I thought until everything came to a halt, and I had to rethink life. In the midst of making a life change that would involve the lives of my three young children, I sat thinking, *Something has to change*, and that change had to start with me. I couldn't continue to do what I always did and expect a different result. On that day, I decided to walk away from my home, my marriage, my comfort zone, life as I knew it. Instantly, I was overcome with questions of how will I survive, what will people think, will I destroy my children, is this a selfish decision—everyone thought my life was perfect, and now I'll look like a failure.

After battling with all of those thoughts, I did something I don't do often: I asked for help. I reached out to my best friend, and I told her I needed to talk. When I arrived to her, I was the most full vessel you could ever encounter. I poured every drop of that pain, heartache, suffering, and stress out of my body, and she cried with me, she laughed with me, and she held me as only a true Sister/Friend could do, and in the midst of her hugging and holding me, I realized it wasn't just the physical act of her holding me; she was spiritually, emotionally, and mentally holding me when I was no longer able to hold myself! After our conversation, she wrote me a letter telling me what a privilege and an honor it was for me to trust her with my pain, that she would never judge me and would always stand by me with any decision I make. I'd always been the reliable friend that everyone could count on, but to know I had that same level of friendship waiting to be reciprocated was the best feeling in the world!

I did follow my decision to leave my home and give my marriage a time to heal; he and I both trusted the healing process and have now been married for 22 years. In the letter my Sister/Friend wrote me when I left home, she chose to add all the things she loved about me. That letter, still today, continues to carry me through some rough times.

I challenge you, my Sisters, to write a letter to each of the sisters in your circle, tell them how you feel about them, what you love most about them, and your most memorable experience! It will change both of your lives!

I dedicate this to My Sister My Friend, Samora R. Taylor. She is gone but never forgotten, and her letter and many notes she left me will continue to be the bridge to carry me across!

— - — - — - — - — - — - — - — - — - — - — - —

Natasha V. Cooper is the creator and founder of M.E.O.W. Is this (ME) Nopause or what? It is an online (Facebook) support group dedicated to all things Menopause—the good, the bad, and the UGLY, and it does get U.G.L.Y! She has worked in the public housing field for the last 26 years; her love of service has kept her in this field, and it has both grounded her and taught her each and every life lesson. Natasha is a certified public housing manager as well as a certified senior housing program housing specialist. Her life work has been dedicated to housing and the empowerment of the underserved. Natasha's lifelong love is acting and writing—she loves the stage first, and foremost, acting is her calling; however, playwriting and the writing of poetry, lyrics, and scripts are also a great part of her passion. Natasha lives by the words "Be a blessing, and you will always be blessed." If there is one thing she can offer with no hesitation and is always willing to give at no cost, it is a LAUGH. If she can do nothing else, she can make people laugh, and she loves it!

Lily in the Valley

Tasha D. Henderson

The Lily flower is a symbol of restoration, a return to happiness and life, a symbol of rebirth and humility.

Hello, sister, my name is Tasha, and this testimony is one of faith, love, and God's strength. This testimonial is only a caption of events and conversations, but I wanted to share because I trust someone will be encouraged to know they are not alone in the darkest valley of their life.

I met a beautiful caramel man on a blind date arranged by my best friend and her boyfriend. He invited me to his family reunion banquet and sent tickets through my best friend and her boyfriend at the time. We ended up talking half the night and prayed that God's will would be done as we exchanged telephone numbers. Fast forward a year, and he asked me to marry him. We were engaged for two years and got married the summer before my last semester in college. Life was beautiful, and I never had experienced such a deep love from any man ever. We were best friends and looked forward to what God had in store for us. I graduated from college the next semester with my bachelor's degree in mathematics. My husband Anthony worked hard at his job as a shipping and receiving manager. After one year of marriage, I welcomed our first-born son Jared into the world.

We settled into our first apartment and worked hard to build a life for our family as we stood strong on our faith in Jesus Christ. The next year, we found out we would be welcoming a beautiful baby girl. We were so excited and shocked at the same time. We thought we would have more time before we welcomed another baby. However, the thought of having another girl in the house was so fulfilling. While I was pregnant, we diligently started looking for a larger place instead of our two-bedroom apartment. We decided to pursue purchasing a townhome. Life was so simple back then. We were busy working and instilling morals and values in our children as they grew. We even decided to home school our children during their preschool years.

After living in our townhome for a couple years, we found out we were expecting another beautiful baby boy. Again, God blessed us with a larger place to live, and we purchased our first single family home. Now, this home would be the place where we would stay and build our roots for the family to end the fruit of our labor as years progressed. During this time, we were celebrating 21 years of marriage. Who knew our lives would change in such a dramatic way? Now in between these years, Anthony had finished his bachelor's degree and had started his master's degree. We were well on our way to planning out our life after the kids left for college. We were going to travel the world and take no captives! Anthony had purchased a sharp and shiny Harley-Davidson motorcycle and was doing the things in life he always wanted to do.

I was accomplished in my career and was traveling for work and leisure until one evening I got a call. Anthony was back at home in New York at school attending in his class for his master's degree program. I was in Atlanta and planning to attend a conference for work. I came back to the hotel room after getting a meal to eat. As I fell off to sleep on the bed with my cell phone next to me, the phone rang—a FaceTime call from Anthony.

"I don't feel good," he said. "I think I need to call an ambulance."

Now, my sister, Anthony is never one to say he doesn't feel good, and calling an ambulance was never requested by him, ever! This guy used to be a personal trainer! His body was strong—and built, might I add, and he never really ever was sick at ALL. So I knew that when he said he needed an ambulance that the situation was definitely a 911 emergency! I asked if anyone was around him to call the ambulance. My heart was sinking, and my stomach was doing flips. My God, please help him, is what I was saying to the Lord God. I talked to Anthony's classmate who was thankfully next to him. He called the ambulance. I immediately hung up and called Anthony's brother who lived not far from the college Anthony attended. I knew in my spirit this would not be a normal trip to the hospital. Pacing my hotel room, I stayed on the phone with my brother-in-law as he entered the ambulance and traveled to the hospital with Anthony. I could hear him yelling, "Anthony, are you with me? Anthony, stay with me!"

"What's going on?" I yelled and screamed crying, knowing something was going badly wrong. I immediately fell to my knees and started to pray fervently. I laid prostrate before God crying, screaming for mercy on us during this time. I called my mother and family and immediately asked for prayer. The surgeon from the hospital called me as I was on another line with family. He said Anthony had a major stroke, and 95% of his brain was bleeding and swelling.

"Tasha," he said, "I need you to make a decision quickly to save his life. I need your permission to remove part of Anthony's skull to stop the swelling and remove the blood."

In that moment, God gave me strength and a vision that He was going to take care of Anthony, and he would be healed. I, of course, asked them to proceed and place take good care of Anthony. The next phone call was the nurse to ask for rights for death if Anthony did not make it through surgery. I couldn't believe what was happening! Most importantly, I couldn't believe my best friend was battling for his life in an instant. He had just dropped me off at the airport that morning at 5:30. I had just spoken to him early in the evening so he could help me set up the hotspot on my cell phone for the conference I had to present at. My God, what happened? I felt like everything in our lives was immediately torn apart.

I needed to get back to New York immediately. My supervisor and conference lead helped me get a flight out of Atlanta within a few hours in the middle of the night. Those hours felt like an eternity.

As I was in flight on my way home, I felt my heart racing and thought I was going to have to call the flight attendant for help. While looking out through the plane window, God gave me the scripture *weeping may endure for a night, but joy comes in the morning*. The sun started to rise in the distance, and I felt God's strength and presence immensely. When I landed, my family was there to rush me to the hospital where there was a room filled with our family and close friends. As I entered the hospital room, my living darling Anthony was lying there with so many tubes and machines that I couldn't count. Although it looked so scary, it was nothing compared to him still being alive and making it through the life-saving surgery. The prognosis was grim as a doctor said, "We will give him three days to see if he will make it through." I knew that in three days God raised Jesus from the dead, and God surely could work miracles in my husband in three days, and He did!

Anthony was in the hospital for two months and in rehabilitation for four months. He had to have one other surgery to remove the childhood defect in the brain that caused the stroke. However, he made it through that surgery as well. Anthony has recovered pretty well with a left-side paralysis, and mentally, he has made a 99% recovery. Although Anthony fights each day to gain more and more strength, he is grateful he still has a beautiful life to still live.

As we look back at 25 years of marriage, we have thanked God for the mountains and valleys that have strengthened our faith, marriage, and family.

I Am My Sister's Keeper

My sisters, God is the "Lily in the Valley" during the difficult life-changing moments we never thought we would endure. The valley is a season that will pass. Continue to behold and focus on the "Lily in the Valley."

- - - - - - - - - - - - - - - - - -

Tasha has been married for 25 years to her wonderful husband. They have three amazingly beautiful young adult children. Tasha is an early college and S.T.E.M. program manager that has facilitated various student and adult professional development and church workshops. Tasha is a woman of deep faith and believes that is her anchor for her life's journey. Tasha is a lifelong learner and has a deep passion for helping women live to their fullest purpose in life. Her second passion is for the fields of S.T.E.M. (Science, Technology, Engineering, and Mathematics). She attributes her firm foundation in S.T.E.M. motivates her love for the youth and their future on every level of their being.

Before her career in education, Tasha was a senior computer database administrator for a major financial industry leader for several years. Tasha has a Bachelor of Science in Mathematics and Physics from Elmhurst University, a Master of Arts in Elementary Education from St. Xavier University, and a Master of Arts in Educational Leadership and Administration from Concordia University Chicago. Tasha studied mechanical engineering at the Illinois Institute of Technology. For several years, Tasha was a S.T.E.M. Leadership Sustainability Fellow for Michigan State University, and currently, Tasha is a Ph.D. student studying Leadership in Educational Technology.

In her spare time, Tasha loves volunteering as a board and committee co-chair for various organizations such as Habitat for Humanity, Catholic Charities, J.U.S.T., and other non-for-profit organizations. Tasha has been a co-author for two S.T.E.M. books and has been featured in several podcast episodes and university publications ranging from African-American History to Black Women in the S.T.E.M. fields.

Strong

Dr. Linda Hodo

Broken, weak, sad, lonely, and quiescent were sentiments that I expressed. I never saw this vexation coming. It was like a tornado that swept across a town and destroyed almost everything in its path. The path was my life.

Have you ever been broken, hurt, sad, or lonely?

I'm sure you have. We've all experienced a devastating circumstance at some point in our lives, and if you've haven't yet, just wait. It's coming. It's coming for sure. And no matter how hard we try to avoid a hurtful faux pas, we can't. It's a part of the anomaly within life, and life had recently dealt me a hand that had me speculating my ability to handle it. I can't say that I was completely destroyed; that wouldn't be the truth, but I was broken, weak, sad, lonely, and unable to get up and move.

I Am My Sister's Keeper

Let me open the transparent windows of my life and share several of the calamitous events from the pages of my book. Not to make you sad or feel sorry for me. There's a reason, so hang in here with me. Can you do that? Thank you!

Where shall I begin? For starters, I've been divorced from the love of my life and father of my oldest children for more than twenty years, and divorced from the second love of my life for ten years, and divorced from several relationships from men whom I thought loved me but didn't. The truth is that I have been divorced, and I haven't been successful at love-relationships after looking for love in all the wrong places and faces despite my desire to love and be loved. You know what I mean? But I'm here to tell you that my past baggage of failed relationships did not and will not break me because I have been *strong*!

Hey, don't worry about your failed relationship or marriage because if you desire to be married, God has a special person just for you. The Bible says, "And the Lord God said, It is not good that the man should be alone; I will make him an help meet for him," (Genesis 2:18), and you dear sister are his help meet. For the brothers in the house, you'll cross paths with your soon-to-be-wife because he that finds a wife, finds a good thing and obtain favor with the Lord. Hello, somebody!

It is not my wish for any mother to experience the loss of a child. It is an episode that replays in your heart and mind over and over until tears find their way from the most personal places of your heart to your eyes to cascade like a waterfall at the most unpredictable times. Some of you understand, for you have also suffered this affliction, or you know someone personally who has walked these streets.

I hear you asking: "Have you lost a child?" Yes, I have. It saddens me to say that eighteen years ago, I was pregnant with twin boys, identical. It was a prayer answered. I was elated because I'd soon be blessed with sons as a mature woman of forty. Yes, forty. As you would guess, being pregnant at forty put me in the "high-risk" category. My body was not happy that I had the audacity to give myself permission to get pregnant (and it was no accident) at forty, and my family as a single mother would be expanded. What a joy!

Having had to fight the majority of my complicated pregnancy to keep my twins safe and healthy, I felt relief when we (my twins and I) made it to the eighth month, the month that they would come into this world. Suffice it to say, that Thanksgiving Day, my boys were ready to meet their mom, and I was ready to look upon their identical faces, hold them tight, and bless God for my miracles.

As the nurses and doctors hovered over me whispering, I knew in my heart-of-hearts that something was seriously wrong. The doctor uttered in an unfamiliar tone, "Linda, your babies are in distress. We have to take them by C-section."

"Okay," I responded. My thoughts were focused on my boys although I had realized that something inside of my body had caused them to become stressed. After the spinal tap, they rolled me into the surgical room to pull my babies into safety. Unbeknownst to me and the doctors, a leakage of blood filled the very space where by babies rested. In other words, my boys were swimming in a pool of blood.

The last words that I heard from the doctors were, "Linda, we have to put you under to stop the bleeding and to save your life." I begged my good friend to go with my boys to watch over them because I knew that God was with me. I began to recite the 23rd Psalm as they put me under. I woke two weeks later to one son, Aramis. My other son, Armani, went to heaven without even being held tightly or kissed on the cheeks by his mommy. Tears are falling as I write this.

I Am My Sister's Keeper

Losing my son shortly after birth without beholding his newborn face, holding him close to me, or telling him how much I loved him devastated my heart more than I knew I could be hurt, but it didn't break me. I had to be strong for my other children and myself. What I knew for sure was that all things work together for good for those who love the Lord, and are called according to His purpose according to Romans 8:28. Because God's word will always be true, I was able to say, "I am **strong**!"

Have you ever gone crazy? I mean literally. I don't mean tired, sick, or frustrated when your nerves have been tried to the fullest. In 2007, I experienced a nervous breakdown as a result of the discrimination, racism, and physical threats on my life that I faced in a toxic work environment that was filled with hatred.

My mind and body started screaming, "Enough" after years of enduring this kind of treatment. I broke out in hives, lost my sight temporarily, started hallucinating, became paranoid, and I could not sleep for weeks at a time. My body literally shut down, my brain went haywire, and I found myself in the hospital. As a nervous wreck, I acted strange, I trusted no one, I was afraid of the dark, and of everything else. I was not myself. As Joyce Meyers would say, it was a battlefield of the mind.

One day while I was in the hospital, the Lord sent an angel, my pastor Dr. Lonnie Dawson, (May He Rest in Peace) with a word to encourage me. He quoted, *"The LORD is my light and my salvation, so why should I be afraid? The LORD is my fortress, protecting me from danger, so why should I tremble?"* (Psalm 27:1)

It was an on-time word that kept me focused and standing on God's word during a true breakdown. Because of the Word, I continued to stand and say, "I am **strong.**"

Just in case you need a word of encouragement and focus because your world seems to be falling apart all around you, focus your mind on whatsoever things are true, whatsoever things are honest, whatsoever things are just, whatsoever things are pure, whatsoever things are lovely, whatsoever things are of good rapport; if there be any virtue, and if there be any praise, think on these things (Philippians 4:8).

Have you seen those commercials where a senior has fallen to the ground in the kitchen or in the bathtub, and they say, "I've fallen and I can't get up"? All of us have, I think. Each time my friends and I saw that commercial, we poked fun and laughed. I guess you could say—or maybe I should say that I'd never thought that falling could happen to me. But, after almost sixty years of life and great health that afforded me opportunities to do everything that I dared to indulge in like dancing, biking, hiking, skating, walking for miles, boating, executing perfect Karate moves, and traveling across the nation and the oceans, *I fell* and broke my right ankle. Not only that, but I also badly sprained my left ankle, leaving me quiescent for the first time in my life.

Suffice it to say, an emergency room visit led to surgery, a knee-high cast on one leg, the other wrapped in ace bandage, and a condition called temporary immobility.

Me, immobile? Say it was not so. Everyone who knew me would attest to the fact that I am high energy, full of joy, and ready for what was next, especially if it involved fun, family, or ministry work. How was such a ball of fire supposed to sit and wait patiently for the healing process of my ankles to run its course? The truth was that I didn't have a choice.

For the first time in my life, *I was broken*. Being literally broken ushered in sadness and loneliness; I was weak and that opened to door for fear to waltz into my life. I was no longer the 'strong woman' I had always been. This state of weakness left me vulnerable, and I felt that I couldn't stand to defend myself, my senior parents, or my youngest son if I needed to.

The weakness in my body spread to my heart and mind. I'd been in a bad place, and no one could see the tears behind my smile.

I was put in position to sit and wait. Sitting for hours upon hours, day after day for several months was definitely out of my comfort zone. To help myself sit (literally), I engaged in self-talk. I told myself over and over, "Be patient with yourself. You can do it."

I also remember asking God why He didn't warn me about the holes in the grass. God didn't answer that question until Sunday, August 16, 2020, three months later. Although He didn't answer my question right away, He did prepare me by telling me to work out and lift weights to strengthen my upper body. I did as He told me to, but I did wonder why He didn't say to work out on my legs. God knew, because He is Omniscience, that I'd have to use my upper body meaning my arm muscles to move from the bed to the floor, to my walker/wheelchair, to the restroom and back to the bed.

For three months, my muscles had become weak. Not just my ankles, but also my dancing feet, my legs, and my arms. I hadn't moved, I mean exercised, in all of that time.

I Am My Sister's Keeper

One morning as I lay in bed, the spirit of the Lord reminded me that I belonged to Him. He shared the fact that He allowed this circumstance to rebuild me to be even stronger in my body, for He had work for me to complete, and that work required strength far greater than I previously possessed. While experiencing the healing process, God opened the door for me to become a certified health/life coach. The Lord positioned me to purchase property. My Father enlarged my women's empowerment territory conference to include men. God strengthened me from the inside starting with my bones, throughout every organ of my body, mentally, spiritually, and socially. I have to tell you that God strengthened my writing and painting hand. God was showing me whom He is during my broken moments during the pandemic, and He has proved to me that when I was weak, He was strong for me. Because God is my strength through the good and the bad, I am *strong*!

The best news is that despite what you have been through, how it felt, what it looked like, how you've cried, how you've felt, or despite the trajectory presented to you right now, "You are strong!" in the power of His might (Ephesians 6:10). God is with you, just as He has been with me through every difficult road I have traversed, and you can *stand strong* and profess His word. His word will carry you through the fire, the storm, the rain, the hurt, and the pain.

Say it with me: "I am strong." Say it again: "I am strong," and because I know that you are professing your strength, that makes me stronger. Amen!

Always Strong!
Dr. Linda Hodo

— · — · — · — · — · — · — · — · — · — · — · —

Linda M. Hodo, EdD is a life/health coach, experienced administrator and teacher who has served over thirty-five years in public education to ensure that students (including adults) in California's inner city realize their educational goals and dreams.

She wholeheartedly believes the adage, "Dreams can come true," especially when addressing today's youth and young adults. It's with this mind-set that Dr. Hodo has awarded academic scholarships since 2008 to young women who are beginning their college journeys. Another avenue for her to support teens is the twelve-week program that she developed based on the book of Esther called, "Women of Excellence," that focuses on etiquette, behavior that reflects a young-Christian woman, and dealing with life issues effectively while having fun.

She makes a concerted effort to take written letters of appreciation to veterans each year to express appreciation for the services they have rendered for our country. Her heart is one that embraces people.

Dr. Hodo is an author. Her most popular brooks thus far are, *Only In My Dreams*, a personal narrative about love, and relationships, and *Fight*, which emphasizes the whole armor of God—the tools for spiritual warfare based on Ephesians. Her goal is to assist her readers to enjoy the world of literature through her stories and encourage everyone to stand strong when facing life challenges.

As a full-time professional, mother, church ministry leader and a caretaker for senior parents, Dr. Hodo relates to the sacrifices that women endure to serve in their all of their life-roles. She realizes the benefits for women of all ages to practice lasting healthy habits to live balanced (healthy) lives and reduce stress. Her service as a Health/Life Coach and her annual "Women's Empowerment" conference features notable artists, entertainers, workshops, services, and products, including health and fitness to assist women in creating habit change by sharing her expertise to foster ultimate health and energy. If you would like to take steps to experience ultimate health and energy in various areas of life, contact Dr. Linda and get started today!

God, Please Help Me Get Through This

Twana
Matthews

On December 28, 2019, I was so happy because I was with my loved ones. My son, daughter-in-law, grandchildren, and I were out shopping. We were at the mall allowing my grandchildren to spend the money that they had received on Christmas.

As we entered the mall, my son and grandchildren went shopping for shoes, while my daughter-in-law and I decided to go to another store. Upon arriving at the store, I received the worst phone call of my life. My sister was calling to tell me that our mother had died.

Hearing those words felt like someone had just hit me in the stomach with a brick. I was devastated. My thoughts were all over the place. My mind was racing. How could something like this happen so suddenly and unexpectedly? Within seconds, my happiness turned into sadness.

I Am My Sister's Keeper

We immediately left the mall and went straight to my sister's house. When we got to her house, my mother's body was still there. The medical examiner advised me not to go into the room where she was. I went against his advice, telling him, "You don't understand. I have to see her."

As I entered the room, I saw her laying on the floor. My mother, whom I loved dearly, was laying there. I can't describe how helpless I felt as I stood there looking at my precious mother. I had been there many times for her during her struggles in life, and we all have them. But this time, I could not help her. So I bent down and kissed her on her forehead for the last time. I said *goodbye for now* to my mother. It was so painful.

Everyone was looking to me for comfort and strength. I pretended to be strong, but no one could see that I was tore up on the inside. I was hurting. My heart was broken. I thought, *How can my heart ever heal from this?*

The day of her funeral, as I was closing the lid of the casket, my legs began to weaken. I felt as though my heart was about to explode. But I had to keep pretending that everything was all right because everyone was looking at me.

When I went home that night, and many nights afterwards, I had no one to hug and hold me and tell me that everything would be all right. I cried myself to sleep many nights. I was in a state of mind that I had never been before. I never imagined or knew that the loss of my dear mother would hurt so badly.

Then one night, as I was crying and saying, "God, please help me get through this," I heard my Lord and Savior Jesus Christ say to me, "I am here with you, and I will never leave you nor forsake you. So let not your heart be troubled." He told me to lean on him for comfort and strength, so I began to lean on the Lord like never before. He brought me through the seconds, the hours, the days, and the weeks.

I am so glad that I am a witness that when you call on God in prayer, He will come see about you. He will give you beauty for your ashes. He will put joy back in your life. He will mend your broken heart. How does He mend your broken heart? He mends it through the Word of God. He heals it through prayer.

You see, sometimes life will throw us a curveball and knock us off our feet. It sometimes sucks the air out of us. In those moments, we need to whisper a prayer. Prayer is so important. It is a way that we communicate to God, and sometimes, we have to whisper a prayer and say, "God, please help me get through this!"

Help me get through this loss of my mother, help me get through this loss of my father, help me get through this loss of my brother, help me get through this loss of my sister, help me get through the loss of my child..."God, please help me get through this!"

So, whatever you're going through, take it to God in prayer. Your situation may not be the loss of a loved one. It may be the loss of a job, or the loss of a home. Your marriage may be on shaky ground, and it's about to fall apart. Perhaps you are experiencing the loss of finances. All of these things can be overwhelming. I know because I have been through every one of them. But the good news is that I also came through every one of them. I came through by holding on to God's unchanging hands through prayer. I kept saying, "God, help me get through this." God brought me through, and he can bring you through, too.

Listen to me, my sister, God is near, so cry out to him. He hears our cry for help. His ears are open to us. Tell him about the rough night you had. Tell him about your troubles. He hears your cry, and he will wipe away every tear. Not only does he hear us, but He also delivers us out of all our troubles. All you have to do is cry out to him and say, "God, help me get through this."

There's nothing too hard for God. Learn to look to God and cry to him. No matter what you are going through or what is coming against you, it's not too big or hard for God. Yes, the pressure is on, and you may sometimes feel like you are not going to make it out. But know this today—God is with you, and you will make it out of whatever situation you are facing.

So be encouraged—God is on your side. I encourage you to pray this prayer, "Lord, I don't understand why I'm going through this trial, but I choose to trust you and to rest in your strength. Thank you for helping me, Lord, to get through this. Amen."

———————————————————————

Twana Matthews is a loving mother of two sons. God has blessed her with six grandchildren and two great-grandchildren. She demonstrates a loving passion for God and people. She is an associate minister, youth counselor and outreach coordinator at Greater Shield of Faith Baptist Church, Detroit, Michigan. She is a member of the NAACP and currently works at Beaumont Hospital as an anesthesia tech. She is a co-author of the #1 bestseller, *Girl Get Up and Win.*

Work Your Plan, Sis!

Dr. Aginah M. Muhammad

"For tomorrow belongs to the people who prepare for it today."
~African Proverb

Life doesn't always go according to plan. Sometimes, we get off course and take a detour that will lead us to a new and exciting destination. We all have dreams and aspirations, whether it's to get married and live happily ever after or have a successful career. We have goals. As a little girl, I had dreams and aspirations of how my life as an adult would turn out. I planned to get married to a successful businessman, have four children (two boys and two girls), become a successful attorney, and live in a nice home in the suburbs. What I've learned over the last several years is that sometimes it's necessary to adjust our plans. It's been seven years since the ink dried on my divorce papers, and while I married a blue collar worker instead of a businessman; had three children instead of four (a set of boy/girl twins and a daughter); and entered the field of higher education instead of law, I can confidently say that I still believe in the "Power of a Plan."

I am sure you were probably like me and dreamed about your wedding day. After all, as women, we are conditioned to aspire to marriage. So many of us fantasize about the day—of having a picture-perfect wedding. In my dreams, my wedding was absolutely perfect. I had a beautiful ring, a stunning dress, an amazing venue, and a dynamic wedding party. I dreamed about my wedding for so long as a young girl that when I became engaged nearly 20 years ago, I knew exactly how my wedding day would go. For the most part, it was exactly as I had planned. We were blessed to have a beautiful wedding ceremony in June of 2002, where my late father had the honor of walking me down the aisle and serving as the officiant.

As a 24-year old, I thought I knew enough to successfully get through the first few years of marriage and more. I also had a great example of what marriage looked like in my parents who, at the time, had been married for 31 years. I thought my husband and I would make plans for our future, and life would be perfect as long as everything went according to my plan. I am pretty sure you had the same goal or something very similar. Right? As little girls, many of us dream about marrying the perfect man, starting a family, and living happily ever after. We become so focused on the wedding day that oftentimes we don't consider what life will be like after we say those two little words: *I Do.*

I was so caught up in planning my wedding that I ignored the red flags that were present in my relationship before I walked down the aisle. In fact, there was a point during our engagement that I called the wedding off. But due to the anticipated embarrassment of what I thought people would say or what people would think about my decision, I decided to go through with the wedding anyway. I also didn't want to disappoint my parents. They were ecstatic about me getting married. Have you ever stopped to ask yourself why we are so focused on planning our wedding day that we don't consider all of the other aspects of marriage? I asked myself this question a thousand times.

During the course of my eleven-year marriage, I tried to work on it. During the first two years, I tried to improve the line of communication, find ways to connect with my husband, and make adjustments in an effort to save the marriage. I wasn't successful. Instead, I began going through the motions. In the midst of going through the motions, we had three children. The last thing that I wanted to do was raise my children alone without their father. Consequently, I remained in a marriage filled with pain and agony much longer than I could have ever anticipated or planned.

I was holding on to a marriage that no longer served me. I held on for the sake of my children, my family and, quite frankly, my ego. I thought that by getting a divorce, I was a failure. I didn't want to be classified as a failure because I was a woman of strength. And since I was a strong woman, I thought I had to hold on to my marriage and the picture-perfect family. After thinking this way for so long, I came across advice given by *Chicago Sun-Times advice columnist*, Ann Landers: "Some people believe holding on and hanging in there are signs of strength. However, there are times when it takes much more strength to know when to let go and then do it." At the age of 35, I had an epiphany. I realized that I could no longer continue to live for others. I had to choose to live for myself. I couldn't continue to hold on to a dream that my marriage would get better. I also realized that *holding on is believing there's only a past. And letting go is knowing there is a future.* The moment that I let go, I began to understand that just because my marriage didn't turn out the way I wanted it to didn't mean that my future wouldn't turn out the way I wanted it to.

I Am My Sister's Keeper

I had a choice to make. To ensure a better future, I had to not only change my way of thinking but plan and prepare. Planning and preparation are two of the most important elements for a successful transition from being married to becoming a divorcee. Planning and preparation will help reduce the stress and uncertainty of life during and after your divorce. Life after divorce is certainly a major adjustment, but I think it goes without saying that it should not be more difficult for women and mothers looking for better lives for themselves and their families.

When I went through my divorce seven years ago, I knew that it was important to plan and prepare. And while I planned and tried to prepare for my divorce, I still learned lessons throughout the process. I had to be strategic, and that's what I want for you. Once you come to the conclusion that filing for a divorce is inevitable, it's important that you have a plan in place. Here are a few tips that I hope you will find helpful as you prepare for your transition.

Make a plan: Make a plan and work on it to take control of your divorce process. Do not let the divorce process take control of you!

Make a to-do list: Staying organized is very important along with setting your priorities during a divorce. List all the items you have to accomplish and mark them off as you go through them.

Conduct your research: While every divorce is different, make sure you learn everything you can about divorce early in the process. Learning about the basics and the ins and outs of the divorce process will help boost your confidence, comfort level, and odds of success with the final outcome. Becoming knowledgeable about the process will help you make the best decisions for your current situation and your future.

Gather financial info & start a war chest: Without question, you are going to need your own money for a divorce. If you're a mom, then you will need to be able to maintain yourself and your children, particularly if you are financially dependent on your spouse. You'll need money to retain an attorney. Make sure you organize your own financial documents that can be used as a checklist and share it with your attorney during your first meeting to save time and expense. If possible, open a separate account to guard against future financial contingencies during the divorce process.

Cut expenses: If you have debt in your name, like student loans or credit cards, pay as much of the debt down as possible before filing for divorce. You will need to cut down on disposable or unnecessary purchases.

Practice self-care: If you want to come out of the divorce process whole instead of wounded, you will need to take care of yourself. You need to make sure that you maintain your health and well-being by eating right, exercising, and getting sufficient sleep. It's going to be challenging, but you will need to carve out time to take care of you. Otherwise, you won't be any good to your children or be able to get through the divorce process without becoming overwhelmed and stressed.

Select a therapist: Divorce is an emotional roller coaster. A therapist can help you to understand your emotions and provide helpful tips on dealing with the myriad issues that will arise throughout the divorce process. Having someone consistently by your side will help you keep a level head and your emotions in check.

Learn to receive & ask for help: As women, we are, by nature, givers. We take care of everyone else first, but we rarely allow anyone to take care of us. If you have a close circle of friends or family members who want to help you through this challenging time in your life, let them. It's okay to receive help from someone who genuinely wants to be there for you.

Get support from your sister circle: Select a core group of friends and family who will be there for you during your divorce. Your group should be large enough where you aren't sharing all of your divorce woes with only one or two people, but small enough to where everyone doesn't know all of your personal business. If you are unable to galvanize a core sister circle, then consider a divorce support group.

Rediscover who you are and don't start dating until AFTER your divorce: Divorce is just a simplified term to describe the death of a marriage. Naturally, you will experience a period of grief. Try to fill the void by doing some of the things that you enjoyed prior to getting married. Try to remember the things that make you happy. Don't jump into a new relationship prior to the finalization of your divorce. Dating during your divorce can complicate the divorce process as well as your life. It's important to take time to resolve your feelings for your ex-husband before becoming involved with someone else. Give yourself an opportunity to heal and start fresh.

In conclusion, if there is one thing you should know about going through a divorce, it's this: *No matter how hard the process is, you must tell yourself that you are going to make it.* A divorce has the potential to leave an emotional scar, but it is nothing to be ashamed of. The scar is evidence that you were stronger than whatever tried to hurt you. If you plan and prepare properly, you will come through the process better than how you entered it. You will recognize the magnitude of the power that you hold. You have the power to write a new story, and it will not look anything like your past. As you embark upon this journey of uncertainty, remember the four steps to achievement are to: **plan** purposefully, **prepare** prayerfully, **proceed** positively, and **pursue** persistently.

Go on and work your plan, sis!

▬ ▪ ▬ ▪ ▬ ▪ ▬ ▪ ▬ ▪ ▬ ▪ ▬ ▪ ▬ ▪ ▬ ▪ ▬ ▪ ▬ ▪ ▬

Dr. Aginah M. Muhammad is a mother, higher education executive, adjunct professor, speaker, leadership strategist, and author of *Women Who Persevere: Navigating Motherhood with Power and Grace.* Dr. Aginah positively impacts the lives of women of color through mentorship and empowerment. A catalyst for women, Dr. Aginah assists women with overcoming obstacles and developing goals to get to the next level. Dr. Aginah helps to transform the lives of women by listening to their concerns and desires and assisting with building realistic and actionable career and life balance goals. Dr. Aginah resides in suburban Chicago with her three children.

Sister, You Are a Blessing!

Monique
Reynolds

My sister, I may never get a chance to meet you, and I may never get a chance to say that I love you personally. We may never get a chance to laugh and cry together, but you are my sister.

In Webster's dictionary, "sister" is defined as "a female who has one or both parents in common with another." You may also define sister as "a female sibling, protector; the one who you share a closeness with that no one else understands; a keeper of secrets, always there to help through thick and thin; a best friend for life." That to me closely defines *sister*.

My sister, you are beautifully and wonderfully made; Our Heavenly Father says that about you and me. Sister, you are a Royal Diadem. I want to encourage you to stay or be strong and courageous as God told Joshua in Joshua 1:9. There is a God that is bigger than anything that we face; there is nothing too hard for God.

I want to take this time and not assume that everyone has a relationship with God and ask if you do not at this time, say a little prayer with me and invite God into your life right now. Say, "Heavenly Father, I come to You in the Name of Your Son Jesus. You said in Your Word, Romans 10:13, that whosoever shall call upon the name of the Lord shall be saved. Father, I am calling on Jesus right now. I believe He died on the cross for my sins, that He was raised from the dead on the third day, and He's alive right now. Lord Jesus, I am asking You now to come into my heart. Live Your life in me and through me. I repent of my sins and surrender myself totally and completely to You. Heavenly Father, by faith, I now confess Jesus Christ as my new Lord, and from this day forward, I dedicate my life to serving Him." If you said this prayer, know that the Angels in Heaven are rejoicing. And hey, sis, so am I.

If you don't have a church home, look for one, and let them know that you have accepted Christ so they can assist you on this journey. Congratulations!

I Am My Sister's Keeper

Hey sis, during this pandemic, seek the face of God. The more you seek Him, the more you will fall in Love with Him. What you are going through, you can give to God, for He will cover you under His wings. My sister, love does not hurt, it does not call you names, discourage you, beat you down. Love protects, provides, encourages, and covers, so seek Him so He can tell you how much you mean to Him. He didn't call you a Royal Diadem for nothing, baby. You are Royalty. Sister, you were born with Royal blood, and you are crowned with Glory and Honor. As you are reading this, He is calling you out of darkness and into His marvelous light.

You may be reading this and saying, "Who is this lady? I don't know her." But, love, know this: God knows you, and that is why you are feeling that tingling in your heart! God has given you dominion and authority.

Sis, take your position and stand with boldness. Straighten your crown and encourage yourself to lift your head up high and walk tall. Be courageous.

My sister, speak to that mountain that has you stagnated, bound, confused, and unmotivated…that is keeping you from seeing what is ahead of you.

My sister, be intentional in what you do, and be careful in what you say, for life and death lie in the power of the tongue, so today, stop speaking negative about who you are. God didn't say that about you! He took His time in creating you! To God, you are more precious than rubies or gold.

Sis, let me tell you something: don't allow anyone tell you who you are, and when they begin to do that, politely remind them who you are. God has plans for you.

Someone out there needs you; they need to hear your testimony, and they need to hear how you overcame. Sis, they can't move forward until you do. I encourage you to move and watch God move.

Don't give up, don't give in, continue to press on.

In 1 John 4:4 (TPT), we read, "Little children you can be certain that you belong to God and have conquered them, for the One who is living in you is far greater than the one who is in the world." So, sis, know that you belong to God, and He loves you, and nothing can separate you from Him.

Sis, you are victorious, you have triumphed over your circumstances, you are not your past, you have overcame, so stop holding on to things that are dead. Let go of the dead weight. As I mentioned earlier, God told Joshua to be strong and courageous, and so I want to reiterate that to you to stay strong and be courageous, for the Lord your God will be with you.

I Am My Sister's Keeper

My sister, remember you are not in competition with your sister. Do not put her down, but encourage her and straighten her crown.

Until next time, you are the best, and this is your year for success!

— · — · — · — · — · — · — · — · — · — · — · — · — · — · —

Monique Reynolds is a mother of 5 (one deceased) and the youngest of 12 siblings. She was ordained as a Teacher of the Gospel in 2019 and is a highly active member of Christ Purpose International Church under the guidance of pastors Apostle Sean and Prophetess Beverly Anike. She is also a member of Crime Survivors for Safety and Justice and has a passion for speaking to women who are seeking God. Monique is the owner of Jewelz Travel and has co-authored a book with several amazing women titled *Girl, Get Up and Win*.

You can reach Monique on Facebook and LinkedIn, handle *Monique Reynolds*.

Sisterhood Saved My Life!

Shay Sane

The day after Christmas, I received the devasting news that my 38-year-old sister Brenda had passed away at home. At the time of the call, I was out visiting a girlfriend. I vividly remember that my body went numb as I told my girlfriend that my sister had just died, and I had to go. I walked out of my girlfriend's house to my car and drove to my sister's house, which was only 20 minutes away; however, that evening, it seemed like it took me two hours. When I finally arrived at her house, I was told that her body was still in her room. After my sister's body was removed from the house, I gathered up my kids, including my sister's 6-year-old son, and packed them into my car. While we were driving home, I overheard my son tell my nephew that now that his mom was gone that I would be his mom now.

I was 29 years old when Brenda died; while I struggled with my daily routine of being a single mother raising two children, my sister Brenda had battled Myotonic Dystrophy, which is form of Muscular Dystrophy. Unlike other types of Muscular Dystrophy, Myotonic Dystrophy does not become a problem until a person reaches adulthood. As a result, there is a reduction in the use of limb movement that prevents a person from walking, dancing, jumping, talking, and even raising their hand. The Brenda I knew was a beautiful, vibrant, fun, loving, outgoing woman—so full of life. I remember watching her dance around the house in excitement every Saturday evening as she was getting ready for a night out with her friends.

ABANDONED BY MY MOTHER & BECOMING A TEENAGE MOTHER

Brenda was not only my sister; she was one of my primary caregivers along with two of my others sisters, Gail and Sheila, when my mother abandoned me when I was 6 years old. My mother gave birth to a total of eight children, and I was the youngest of seven. When I was 8 years old, my sister Terrie and I were sent to live with my sister Sheila, her husband, and three children in an efficiency apartment. The apartment that we lived in was only one room with a small kitchen area in the corner and a bathroom. The bathroom had a sink, toilet, and standup shower. Since the apartment was so small, the shower was used for storing our clothes, and we had to use the sink to clean our bodies. Having no use of a shower, I often went to school smelling and was teased by others.

While living with my sister Sheila, my father would come to visit my sister Terrie and I sometimes. My relationship with my father was estranged due to the volatile relationship he had with my mother due to his alcoholism. Occasionally, Terrie and I would take the public bus to my father's house to get money from him for food. During our visits to my father's house, he would often get drunk and have arguments with his friends and then pass out. Terrie and I would then sneak out of his house to return to my sister's apartment. This pattern continued for about a year, and then my sister and I went to live with my father after he completed a rehabilitation program for Alcoholics Anonymous.

Although the living conditions with my father got better, other things got worse as my father worked two jobs to support us. We also lived in a house with his girlfriend (stepmother) and her daughter and brother. My stepmother was often extremely mean to me and my sister. She treated us differently from her daughter and would deny us food when my dad was not home.

I recalled my stepmother and father frequently got into arguments when we would tell him how she was treating us. As a result of the fighting between them, we stopped telling our father what was going on. When I was approximately 12 years old, my stepmother's brother began touching me inappropriately, and in exchange for my silence, he would give me food or money. During this time, I began to have problems at school, would regularly run away from home, and became extremely promiscuous. To help me with these issues, my father took me to see a psychiatrist once a month. Most of my conversations with the psychiatrist centered around my lack of relationship with my biological mother.

At the age of 15, I gave birth to my first child. My involvement with my daughter's father was purely sexual as we were not in a relationship. Having a child gave me responsibility that I was not prepared for, but I was determined not to abandon her like I had been. My daughter became my focus in life, and although I struggled, I was determined to graduate from high school on time. During my senior year in high school, I had a part-time schedule, which allowed me time for a part-time job that enabled me to support my daughter. After graduating from high school, I moved out of my father's house and into my own apartment while holding down a job in gourmet fast food. The female manager at my job was instrumental in encouraging me to seek higher education or obtain vocational training. I entered a training program that prepared me for a job with the federal government, and after six months of training, I obtained an entry level position in 1990. Once I entered the federal workforce, I was exposed to various opportunities and people who would offer me support and career advice.

DEALING WITH DEPRESSION & FINDING MY SELF-WORTH

While working full-time, my thirst to succeed became my focus, and I entered the paralegal studies program at the University of Maryland. A few years later, I began dating the nephew of a coworker who was also a governmental employee. On the surface, he checked all the boxes for me, and we decided to move in together. One year later, I became pregnant with my second child, and during my pregnancy, my relationship with my child's father became toxic. Six weeks after giving birth to my son, I had to return to work, and my sister Shelia came to stay with me during the week to help me with my children. The breakup with my child's father contributed to unresolved issues with my mother resurfacing and led to a serious bout of depression. This was the darkest time in my life as I isolated myself from most of my family and friends, and I felt extremely hopeless. It was during this time that I knew I needed professional help, so I started seeing a therapist to help me deal with my problems.

In 1998 when my sister Brenda passed away, she was living with my mother as she had been bedridden for the past ten years of her life. I was forced to have a conversation with my mother about burying her daughter, and in that moment, for the first time ever, I saw a pain in my mother that opened my heart to forgiving her for abandoning me. I told her I forgave her and was there to help with whatever she needed me to do. My mother allowed me to make all the burial arrangements for my sister, which allowed me to start my healing journey with her. In addition to her 6-year-old son, Brenda left behind an 18-year-old son who was mentally impaired. I allowed my mother and two nephews to come live with me and my two children. One year after my sister's death, I planned a trip for my entire family including my mother to Disney World for Christmas with the hope of alleviating additional grief for everyone. Annual trips to Disney World became a part of my family's tradition. In addition to trips with my family, I began to take solo trips during times of extreme stress and depression. Travel allowed me to build confidence and discover my self-worth.

Over the years, I have traveled to various islands in the Caribbean including Jamaica, St. Croix, Puerto Rico, St Lucia, St. Thomas, and Turks and Caicos. Through my travels, I was able to tap into power and strength that I did not know I had, which opened further healing from stress at work, from being a single mother, from toxic relationships, from divorce, from grief, and much more. As a begin to evaluate my purpose in life, I wanted to help other women deal with similar traumas and struggles. I later became a certified travel professional to learn how to facilitate trips for groups.

BUILDING A MOVEMENT

In 2014, I created Black Girls On The Go, formerly Black Girl Travel Movement, to empower black women to explore the healing power of travel and strengthen the bonds of sisterhood. Currently, BGOTG is a global travel brand with over 28,000 members, and it generates nearly $1 million in sales and revenue annually.

Shay Sane, the founder and executive director of Black Girls On The Go (BGOTG), empowers black women to heal from racial trauma, depression, domestic violence, personal insecurities, health disparities, and financial abuse through travel.

Before commencing her work with BGOTG, Shay was a certified travel professional and focused on planning luxury travel vacations for women and their families. After a successful career as a travel professional, Shay utilized her travel expertise and personal experience to create a Facebook group in 2014 to provide black women with a safe space to discuss, plan, and explore the healing power of travel. To date, the BGOTG Facebook group has organically grown and has over 29,000 members worldwide.

Tears in a Bottle!

Theresa Simpson

Tears in a bottle is the title of my life story these days. I have shed so many tears over many years, as I am sure so have many of you, but I believe no one seems to suffer or shed more tears than a parent who has to watch their child in pain. Whether it be in illness or death. I believe watching your child suffer and not being able to do anything is the worse suffering one can endure, at least that is how my heart felt as it was breaking apart. This began my journey of solitude with the book of Psalms.

While in the custody of his enemies, David wrote, "You have kept count of my tossing's; put my tears in your bottle" (Psalm 56:8, ESV). David was going through a difficult time. He begins this sad psalm with the words "Be gracious to me, O God, for man tramples on me; all day long an attacker oppresses me" (Psalm 56:1, ESV). The Philistines had captured David in Gath—David was, at the time he wrote this psalm, a prisoner of war, and he had reason to cry and be sorrowful. David says that his struggles are recorded in God's book (verse 8), and he asks God to put his tears in His bottle. What does this poetic language mean? Does God really have a bottle where all our tears go? Are the events of our lives really written in a book?

The idea behind the keeping of "tears in a bottle" is remembrance. David is expressing a deep trust in God—God will remember his sorrow and tears and will not forget about him. David is confident that God is on his side. He says, in the midst of this troubling time, "This I know, God is for me" (Psalm 56:9, ESV) and "In God I trust; I shall not be afraid. What can man do to me?" (verse 11, ESV). God remembers all the things that happen in our lives, including the suffering endured for His sake. In fact, there are many instances in scripture of God's recognition of man's suffering. God is a tender-hearted Father, one who feels and weeps with us. This should be no surprise. God remembers our sufferings and has promised to more than compensate (Matthew 19:29, ESV).

LIVING WITH A STRANGER WHO LOOKS LIKE ME

It is scriptures like these that give me hope and tell me I am not alone. These days, my tears over flow, and I need many bottles to be filled. God's bottle for us is infinity with our tears, it never ends. He knows all our sorrows, he knows our ins and outs before we even get into them, including our children. So, why am I going through this impossible situation where I am living with a stranger who has me second-guessing who I am? I am supposed to be super woman who wears a cape, who is able to leap tall mountains, who is able to overcome any and everything. I am the sista who was told I would never amount to anything but is a first-generation college graduate who graduated with honors, who walked limping across the stage with a patch over her eye and her arm in a sling due to domestic violence days before and was able to get up and say "not" this time because I knew I had the love of two little boys counting on me to succeed. Now both of those boys who are men today are counting on me not to give up on them. That super woman cape is getting thin, however. It has traveled many valleys, one being the valley of single motherhood. Yes, I had my challenges, but I weathered the storms without any doubts no matter how hard. Today, there is a storm that has turned into a tornado; it has been twisting out of control for some time but found its way into my home with a stranger who looks like my son. For months, I have had to watch my son fight and argue and sometimes get so full of rage, where I would literally be backed into a corner and found myself praying and binding spirits such as strife, rage, anger, confusion, rejection, abandonment, and accusations to get off him daily. In my son's opinion, I had become the mother from hell. Yes, being a mother and watching her son fight for his life, all at the same time fighting you as you try to help him in this battle against his mind, body, and soul is truly emotionally exhausting.

THE BATTLE

The battle I fight is PTSD, Post Traumatic Stress Disorder. This is a life-altering mental health condition that's triggered by terrifying event(s)—either experiencing them or witnessing them. It is known to cause flashbacks, nightmares or unwanted memories of the trauma, and severe anxiety, as well as uncontrollable thoughts about the event. The symptoms can last for months or years, and it is known to completely disrupt one's life. Sadly, there is not enough information out there for those who actually live with someone who is suffering with PTSD, and the effects it has on them and their family. I am a mother who knows the effects; I live them daily. My son teaches me daily new ways to cope with him when he is in a crisis situation. For example, when he is out of control, I don't argue with him. It's not about who is right or wrong but being the more rational one and knowing how to pick your battles and walking away from a very uncomfortable situation. All the while, I am caring for him through the night terrors and screams until 3 a.m. while praying God gives me strength. I have been in the mental health field for years, but nothing could have prepared me for such mind-blowing symptoms. He was even put at higher risk factor being in jail; that increased his trauma and exposed him to multiple traumas, which added to his mistrust. Now, his mind plays tricks on him about everyone including the people he loves. Sad to say that medication has been a Band-Aid for him, not a solution. There is no textbook that can tell this mother who has watched her family being torn apart by mental illness to just get over it, cut the apron strings, give him tough love, or give him a pill. Nothing is going to stop the tears I shed into that bottle as I watch my son suffer; somedays, I may even feel helpless, but I refuse to give up.

NEVER GIVE UP

Although the journey continues daily, I will not give up, and I have to remember a very important survival skill and that is to take care of myself first or I won't be around to help my son or anyone else. I have to be intentionally aware of how being in stressful situations can emotionally and physically drain you. I have to stay revived just to keep going. I do this by pouring into myself with positive affirmations, and I reach out to my sisterhood to those who I know will pour into me with positive encouragements, wisdoms, and prayers. I do this so I don't give up and I can continue in this race with my son. Just as King David in the Bible, I am aware I am a prisoner of war, and I need to put my trust in God because only he can understand my true sorrow. Why? I am tossing and turning and shedding tears every day. I have to believe in my soul that God is with me and will not leave me and will get me through each day because he sees who really has me and my family captured and it isn't the Philistines; it's a mental health issue(s).

TEARS NOT IN VAIN

Though, I cry, I know my tears are not futile. God knows each of His children intimately, and every tear I shed has meaning. I trust and believe God remembers my sorrow as if He kept each tear in a bottle. So, now when I pass through a hard-deep valley with tears, I know God is using that valley experience so I can be a blessing to others. Therefore, look for God in your valleys because those who sow with tears will reap with songs of joy (Psalms 126:5).

WORDS OF WISDOM

As you have read my story and heard the challenges that I have endured within my family with PTSD, if I can give any sound advice to any of my sisters who may be experiencing any similar issues it would be:

- To "always" see the person first and the disability second.
- To "never" get so caught up on what is wrong with the individual that you forget that they are a human being who happens to be suffering with a mental illness, who still deserve kindness, care, support and love.
- Do not be a shame or afraid to ask for help and always take care of yourself.

Theresa Simpson is a well-established veteran in the field of therapeutic recreation therapy with over 20 years of experience in both physical rehabilitation and mental health. She is noted for her tireless efforts as a behavioral specialist working with adults and children suffering from traumatic and emotional victimizations. With over two decades of clinical care, Theresa prides herself in the advocacy of educating and empowering individuals to overcome adversity by guided participatory experiences that address health and quality of life. In addition, Theresa is a recognized author of the book *The Power of God's Love*, which addresses the healing of the inner child and focuses on the process of fulfilling and walking in your life's purpose. Her experiences, education, clinical practice, and grounded spiritual being have afforded her the opportunity to assist individuals on their spiritual paths in life. Theresa has not been the typical clinician in her field; she has always had an open heart, a listening ear, and without judgment and believes in giving individuals a voice. You can say she has always been a sister's keeper, so being a co-author of *I Am My Sister's Keeper* gave her a voice.

The Characteristics of a Sistar's Keeper

Donna Taylor

What are the characteristics of a Sistar's Keeper?

I hope you noticed the spelling I am using for the word *sister*, for I not only see you all as sisters but I also see all women as Super Stars, so I call them *Sistars*.

My Name is Donna Taylor, I am an only child, and I did not grow up around close family members, which was not always a good experience for me, especially at holiday time. So for me, that gave me a lot of time to think about what kind of friend I wanted and wanted to be.

I am a licensed cosmetologist, specializing in natural hair and skin and holistic massage; a certified vegan and raw food chef, specializing in juice therapy with a focus on healthy hair and skin; and a trained birth and postpartum doula and ordained minister, specializing in spiritual healing using mirror and herbal work. I worked for Michigan State University for 15 years as a breast-feeding counselor and nutrition educator. I remember one Sunday at church God spoke to me saying that I would till the land, plant the seed, and reap the harvest. At that time, I thought I was going to be a gardener, but God or Universe had another way to till, plant, and reap: through the healing of women from the inside out.

A Reason for the Season

The first thing we must realize is that everyone we come in contact with has a reason to be in our lives: to teach us something or to learn something from us, so I suggest that as a keeper of our Sistars we must have patience and a kind, gentle spirit. A Sistar Keeper should have a listening ear and not be judgmental when one of the Sistars begins to pour her heart to them. I remember a time, while working with a Sistar teaching her about basic nutrition, when she told me that she was just out of prison, and how her and her boyfriend robbed a bank and that they would have gotten away with it if the boyfriend had not told someone what they had done. She spoke about how much fun she had doing it, and if she could get away with it, she would do it again. While she was telling me this story, I just listened with amazement, for I knew she needed to get the story off her chest. The thing I learned from her is that life is too short do what brings you complete and utter joy and never regret doing so. If a criminal can put trust in what they do, then I should not have any fear in doing things that I know God is leading me to do for the good of others.

Mirror Mirror

A Sistar Keeper should remember that we mirror each other, which means if your Sistar is being mean, sarcastic, or downright b*****, you have, too. That presents an opportunity for you to love the hell out of your Sistar, remembering that love covers a multitude of sins. Having said that, a Sistar Keeper should be loving at all times. I remember working on a project with a young lady, four other people, and the project manager. All of us complained about how the manager was running the project—some complaints we expressed to the manager, and some we did not. The young lady complained as well, but she would go and tell the manager everything we said and not the things she was saying, so over time I built up some animosity against this young lady because she admitted that she was a brown noser. Fast forward a short time later, and I ran into to this young lady while working with her on another project, and I still had animosity against her. Every day, she would come in and tell me how much she liked me and how great of a person I was, and in return, I would tell her that I don't like her very much, and this went on for weeks. Then things began to change in me; I began to see the young lady through different eyes. By the end of the project, I could honestly say I had nothing but love for her, and to this day, we are friends. Actually, I call her family. She loved the hell right out of me.

Sometimes, as a Sistar Keeper, you may have to be in the background as silent support while your Sistar is shining bright before the nation. I have the honor to be friends/sistars with some incredibly talented women, and sometimes, they need some sistarly advice. Some they take. Others ignore. I have given some advice that has catapulted some of those friends/sistars to the next level in their lives. Sometimes, I would get recognition or thanks, and sometimes, they would act as if I did nothing to assist, which is fine, for I am happy to be able to help.

Tough Love

Sistar Keepers have to lovingly administer some tough love, being as gentle as possible. Sistar Keepers should be trustworthy. Sistar Keepers should protect their Sistars mentally and spiritually. There are times when you know you Sistar is completely out of line, and because you love her, you help her to see the error she is making and show her some other options she could take that are healthier.

As I write down these characteristics, I can hear people say it is impossible to have all of these qualities, but I need you to understand that you can develop them all with patience and perseverance.

How do *I* keep myself in line so *I* can be a great Sistar Keeper?

- Pray and meditate daily for at least 30-60 minutes a day.
- Read scriptures twice a day before I start my day and before I go to bed.
- Listen to and recite positive affirmations daily as needed.
- Look at myself in the mirror and tell myself how much I love and adore me.
- Make sure I remember the four agreements by Don Miguel Ruiz:
    - Be impeccable with my words.
    - Don't take anything personal.
    - Don't make assumptions.
    - Always do your best.

Donna Taylor is a licensed cosmetologist specializing in natural hair and skin care; a certified vegan/raw food chef specializing in juice therapy, trained birth, and postpartum doula; and a certified minister since 2016; her focused area is rebirthing women into the superstars they are was born to be and using the skills I have acquired over the year. "We as women," Donna says, "must understand that we are mirror reflections of each other, the Good, the Bad, and the Ugly. So we need to stop judging one another and learn to embrace and love each other."

The Journey to Becoming My Sister's Keeper

Queen Turner

Why am I my "sister's keeper"?

Because I was kept by some great influential people in my life, such as Zsa Zsa Gábor, Isaac Hayes, and Ike Turner to name a few, and me, being blessed, I was always taught to pay it forward, wanting to make a difference to someone's life with my knowledge of not just survival, but living my life like it's golden, to know what it is to be rich and poor, but always knowing that there is light at the end of the tunnel, and to know their worth because for others to know it we've got to show it.

I Am My Sister's Keeper

My journey to becoming my sister's keeper began when I was very young and contained many valleys and some mountains. It would be the valleys that would call me to better myself… and help to better my *sisters*.

I was born into a family of teenage parents: Posie Turner (17) and Queen Hunt-Turner (13). My paternal grandmother Annie Mae Turner was also there. At 6 years old, I experienced my first birthday party, one that was full of my parents, family, and their friends. My siblings were sent to bed, and the spotlight was on me. I sang and danced the night away until my Grandma said, "Enough, Queen. And Posie, this child has got to go to bed. She's already too grown for her age."

All the adults were clapping and asking for more, and I knew then I wanted to be an entertainer. That entertainment bug bit me. Now, fast forward to my preteen years. I was very mature for my 11 and a half years of age. My mom, the older Queen, would come to me for advice about life because I was very knowledgeable at that time. I was singing with a young female group of hood-girls, Ivy & The Ivylettes. We sold out major venues in the DC, MD, and VA better known as DMV. When the tensions started in the group, after an incident about *The Ed Sullivan Show*, my dad, who was my manager, knew my mother's brothers and sister had a group called Pedro and the Soul Runners, and I was added to the group. We became another hot item in the DMV. Boy, did I relish the praise and spotlight.

That praise would diminish by the end of my 12th birthday because I became pregnant with my first child. While pregnant, my grandmother told me how young my mother was when she had me. That reveal caused a growing tension between the two. Things became so tense at home that my grandmother decided to move back to North Carolina. After being with me all my life, she was ready to get away from my parents as she did not approve of the way I was treated after the baby.

I found myself alone with a daughter and no grandma. My moody parents were starting to have marital issues, many of them stemming from being so young when they married. My parents had physical custody of my daughter during those days. It was standard if the child who gave birth was a minor. Although I didn't want to leave her, at 14, I ran away and promised my daughter I would return to get her. I could not live with my feuding parents any longer, and in my young mind, I figured I would have a better life without the mistreatment.

I Am My Sister's Keeper

For a year, I was on my own, and at 15, I met a 20-year-old Air Force recruit who I fell madly in love with, or so I thought. We married just months into our relationship, and in short time, I became pregnant, he went to Vietnam, and I went to his hometown of Houston, Texas, to prepare for the birth of our daughter, my second child. After giving birth and him coming home from Vietnam, things were never the same, and our happy marriage did not last very long.

One of my uncles, who I performed with in DC, was now one of the famous Bar-Kays out of Stax Records, Memphis, Tennessee. When he performed in Houston, he told me that the singer Isaac Hayes was looking for dancers. I left my second daughter with my in-laws and boarded a bus to Memphis, where I auditioned and got the job. Now, I was being groomed and mentored by a famous musician, the " Black Moses" himself. Isaac Hayes, Bubba as he was affectionately called, saw my potential and my talent after traveling with his group around the world.

After winning an Academy Award for the music soundtrack of *Shaft*, Isaac was bitten by the acting bug and decided he wanted to act. He asked me what I wanted to do, and I said, "I can't go home because I'm a runaway." He called his friend, Don Cornelius, the creator of *Soul Train*, whom I had met during his hosting of the Jesse Jackson Push Expo. I went to see Don in California, and the rest, as they say, is history. I was 16.

While dancing on *Soul Train*, I met a Hungarian film and TV director by the name of Ivan Nagy Ivonne, who had some famous home girls who turned out to be the infamous Zsa Zsa Gábor and her sister Eva. Zsa Zsa took me under her wing and groomed me to learn how to play with the rich people. I was a fast learner, but I just picked the wrong ones.

Zsa Zsa was a great mentor, but Ivan turned out to be not so great, and when I would not play the game, in stepped Madam Heidi Fleiss who became the sacrificial lamb. Thank you, Zsa Zsa Gábor. After traveling the world with various groups, I met Eric Monte, the creator of *Good Times*, and the movie *Cooley High*. We had a great relationship, but when he let the powers that be mess with his money, our relationship soured. During one of my trips, off the road performing, I was asked to come to Ike and Tina Turner's Bolic Sound Studios. After working with Ike for a few days, we were talking about our last name, and he said I favored some of his family. My paternal grandfather's name came up when he advised me my grandfather was his cousin. My grandpa and Ike's dad were preachers, and then I realized those times my grandfather was absent from home. He was in Mississippi with another whole family. Ike became a great mentor until the drugs got the best of him, but he always looked out for me.

While in California, I gave birth to two more children, two boys. The family of my oldest son's father were very prominent people in the community. Life was not always peaches and cream, but I could take lemons to make lemonade after being poisoned by my husband. I took my sons and fled after he went to prison—for hardly no time at all. It was then that I began to evaluate my worth and knew I needed more than a GED to provide for my children. They had never wanted for anything, and I didn't intend for them to start now. Thanking God for letting me survive, I vowed to help other women not to stay in a broken relationship just because they don't think they were worthy of fulfilling their needs and goals.

So, in order for me to help someone, I had to start helping myself. I enrolled in mortuary college and became one of the best female embalmers in LA County. After years of raising my children, even after adopting a daughter, I started counseling women of domestic violence, helping them relocate and get back on their feet. When my back became too unbearable to stand on concrete, I did various corporate jobs, but they didn't pay enough, so I purchased adult entertainment business and pursued that instead. I've since created my own reality TV show, *Diva Glammas* about modern day grandmothers. Our motto is "We age up, BUT we don't age out." All my divas have their own moniker according to their personalities. The show is based in the clothing store Front Page Fashion 1 - Home of the Diva Glammas in Palmdale, California, owned by myself and my classy diva and business partner, Elizabeth Camilo. We're currently shopping for a new network for the show. Elizabeth and I also have a non-profit donating clothes to women who are trying to get back to work or school, and BookBags for Kids.

— · — · — · — · — · — · — · — · — · — · — ·

The saying "Queen of the Crop," which is my spin on *cream of the crop*, means *Top of the Line*; it is the best way to describe me because I know I have to hold myself to high standards and think highly of myself in order to achieve greatness.

My book, *Queen of the Crop* will be out by winter 2020. I love you all, and you all know who you are.

What's in a Name?

Dr. Tracy
Washington

My parents named me Tracy; today, my children call me Mom; my best friends call me Sis; and my students call me Professor Washington, and yes, these are all a part of me and who I am, but years ago in my marriage, I was never called by any of the names I listed above. I was called stupid, dumb, ugly, and his most favorite name was Bitch. Before I get too deep into my story, let me tell you a little about my background. I was self-conscious and unaware of my potential since all of my dreams, my desires, and my life were controlled by my parents. Vowing to break free from controlling parents and stepping out on faith to live my life was my way of being grown and rebellious, and then... he came into my life. This guy who wanted to marry me, make all of my dreams come true, and ensure that I was the happiest person in the world. I gladly accepted his marriage proposal. Throughout the years, we managed to have a family, a house, several cars to drive, and money in the bank. He was a true gentleman who held true to his words until that cold rainy night when I did not respond to his question quick enough. To this day, I am still trying to remember the question that changed my world. My life of being happily married was no longer my life. I had suddenly become a battered wife and mother. I had never felt the hand of hatred before in my life. As a child, I have been hit by my parents, I have even gotten into a few fights with my siblings, but to feel a fist connect with my face from a man who once promised me the world was different: unwelcomed… unnecessary… and unbelievable.

I knew I had to escape this situation. Between the harsh words and the physical abuse, I was determined to never let my ex-husband's vulgar words define me, so I left my abusive marriage. Leaving my marriage left me single, broke, a mom to three young children, and the extra income I had become accustomed to had now decreased to one income...my income. Life was hard, depressing, and frustrating; I was tired of working dead-end jobs, sometimes two jobs, as I tried to make ends meet because I did not receive child support. Did I regret leaving the marriage? Heck no! My sanity was well more important to me than an extra paycheck in our bank account.

Stepping Out on Faith

In my frustration and ranting, I remember expressing to my kids how important it was to expand your education beyond a high school diploma. I wanted them to do and be better than I was currently doing for myself. I mentioned to my oldest son that he would go to college and obtain a degree, and his exact words to me were, "Why, Mom? Why do we have to get a college degree when you do not have one?" And to be honest, he was correct; I could not argue with him. He had a point. As parents, we should set an example for our children to follow, so I decided to enroll back in school. Now let me be very clear, nothing had changed in my life. I was still a single parent, I was still broke, I was still working at my dead-end job, but I needed to make a change not only for my children but also for myself. So in January 2010, I enrolled in college to obtain my bachelor's degree in human services.

The journey was scary and exciting all at the same time, but I was not going to let fear prevent me from accomplishing my goal. One thing I have learned as an adult, you will always have family and friends in your corner when they are doing better than you are doing (financially, mentally, and even emotionally). However, as soon as you begin to work on improving and elevating yourself, you lose people along the way. I obtained my degree in two years, and I will say it was a feeling that I cannot explain. I had accomplished a goal that I had tried to do so many times when I was married, but it never happened because "something" always came up, but I did it…I graduated with honors. Once I completed my bachelor's, I said to myself, hmmm, this was a great feeling, I wonder how I would feel if I keep going, and that's exactly what I did.

I immediately enrolled in the master's program at an online institution, and within two years, I obtained my Master's in Business Administration with a concentration in Finance. When I tell you, people left me, my friends claimed I changed, my family did not want to be associated with an "educated" woman, but through all of my ups and downs, my kids never left me; in fact, they were the best support system I had, and that was all I needed in my life. Obtaining an educational degree is the one thing no one can ever take away from you, so after completing my second degree, and feeling the self-gratification, I prayed and asked God to show me what else I should do, and before I could second-guess myself, I enrolled in the doctoral degree program. I mentioned I had lost family and friends; well I have discovered, the higher you go in life, the more you lose those who were never really in your corner from the beginning. I completed my degree in two years; apparently, two was always my magic number. I completed three degrees in six years. Can you imagine how amazing I felt hearing my name being called as I walked across that stage to participate in the hooding ceremony and receive my degree? Yes, the same girl who was called stupid, dumb, and ugly was now a DOCTOR.

Reinventing Myself

Today, I am a college professor, a published author, a motivational speaker, and I am not any of those mean and evil names he once called me. I am Dr. Tracy Washington, and I was able to restore my peace and push through to make a better life for myself and my children. I overcame adversity, and I no longer doubt myself, my thoughts, or my actions. With the right support system, you can and will achieve all of your heart's desires. You will have the courage to look yourself in the mirror every day and smile. Be proud of who you are, who you have become, and remember every day is a new day. Your mind can play the meanest tricks on you sometimes, but you have to be strong even on those days when you want to stay in bed and pull the covers over your head. You have to shift your mindset and embrace life…your new life. I would be lying to you if I did not mention how afraid I was to keep moving, and of course, some days were hard, but I had to continuously tell myself keep pushing, keep moving, keep going, and it was okay if I fell—as long as I did not stay down long. I had to quickly pick myself up and keep moving. Never look back in your rearview mirror; let the past stay in the past. Losing family and friends along the way helps to open doors for new extended family and friends. Remember, your past does not determine your future, and when all else fails, take a moment out of your day and talk to God. He will never tell you wrong, and He will never leave you. You only get one life; never let anyone dictate how you live YOUR LIFE.

Originally from Charleston, South Carolina, Dr. Tracy L. Washington is a graduate of Walden University where she obtained her Doctorate in Business Administration-Finance. Currently employed as a full-time assistant professor, she teaches finance and business courses on the graduate level. *S.E.X.: She Is a Force to be Reckoned With…* is her first published book.

Being an educator, an author, a dedicated volunteer, and a motivational speaker allows her the opportunity to do the things that are dear to her heart (helping others). In her spare time, she enjoys reading, traveling, and dedicating her time to Zeta Phi Beta, Inc. Sorority. Tracy is a mother to three adults and a grandmother to a beautiful baby girl.

Life Teaches Us, Thank God!

Nydia S. Wells-Evans

Sitting here reminiscing about the past, I realize that life sure knows how to get your attention.

Can you imagine loving someone that in your mind is crazy? I mean he has multiple personalities or something.

At first, being with him was amazing. We spent all our time together; even going to the restroom was not done alone. I thought it was cute at the beginning. Because I felt unwanted, unaccepted, and not loved for so long, having someone who wanted to spend so much time together was absolutely amazing to me. And it made me feel so special, too. He even wanted to dress alike, which was shocking because he was a hood nigga. Yeah, those were the ones I liked, them hood niggas. To be honest, I don't even know how we got here. You see, I wasn't looking for a relationship. I was interested though. My mom moved on the block, and the first time I saw him, I was intrigued. He was fine, had a nice swag, and seemed very cocky, or shall I say arrogant. My God, I was melting in my chair! After about a month or two went by, this nigga had the audacity to speak to me. I was nervous, so I pretended not to hear him. But that didn't stop him though. He spoke again. Then he came closer and let me know he was talking to me.

I was sitting on the steps with my sister and daughter. This was crazy because usually when I am anywhere with my sister, the guys choose her over me. She is a red bone with a nice shape, and me, on the other hand, I am a dark complexion with a thick body. And at that time, I had very little to no self-esteem. I thought that keeping a man around meant I had to do whatever he wanted. I have had my fair share of run-ins with the likes of niggas, which is why I say I wasn't looking for a relationship. I was more of a hit it, quit it, and never look back type of chick in those days. Ironically though, he and I had a long, interesting conversation that night. We also did other things, but the conversation is what mattered most to me. Yes, I did say we did other things, so I thought that would be the last I'd see him in my personal space. But boy was I wrong. I guess he felt the same connection as I because the next day he was asking what time we were going home. I was a little confused, but I answered him none the less by saying, "Maybe 8."

From that day forward, we became inseparable. It's like we were joined at the hip. He spoiled me, wined and dined me, and made sure I was good by any means necessary.

But you know what they say: if it seems too good to be true, it probably is. About three months in, we began arguing. At this point, it was my fault because after being hurt several times in the past, I kind of created a ninety-day rule for myself. In my mind, it was a safety mechanism. The closer we got to ninety days, the dumber shit I would do. Usually it worked, and dudes would just fade away into goodbye 'ism. But for some reason, it didn't work with him. By this time, we were saying I love you daily, and for some reason, I believed him every time he said it. This meant he wasn't going anywhere. While I was thinking it, he said it out loud. For a second, I thought he had the ability to read my mind. Nah, I was just tripping.

A few more months passed by, and yes, we were still together, but now it was just him, myself, and my daughter. See, he was working his magic all around the board, and I was so lovestruck that I wasn't even paying attention. We were about to make one year in a couple of days, and I had no one to call, text, or even celebrate with. I had no one because he had isolated me from everyone, and because they respected my feelings for him, they let us be. So, this is what happened, every time my phone rang, he was arguing in the background. When someone knocked on the door, he was complaining. Even when I used my computer, he accused me of cheating. And since I never felt wanted before him, I just accepted everything he dished out because he made me believe that no one else would want or even love my black, fat, out of shape, and boring ass. He made me feel so small that I didn't even want to be bothered with myself. I stopped doing a lot of the things that I used to before meeting him because he told me that I was wasting my time. I loved him, so I listened not knowing that I was just feeding into his little game the entire time. Now that I looked an absolute mess every day, nobody would want me for sure now. So, he was winning.

I began to notice the patterns of what had happened, and I started to question myself. I was wondering what had happened to me. I used to be so happy and full of life, but now I dreaded waking up in the morning. I was never looking forward to the now norm of hiding bruises, arguing daily, fighting, etc. You see, he had been preparing me from day one, and I never realized it until it was too late. We started with the arguing three months in. I should have walked away then, but I felt like I couldn't because I loved him. Eventually, the arguing turned into fighting every now and then. Then, the "every now and then" turned into every day and, sometimes, more than once a day. I was not making eye contact with anyone other than him. I wouldn't talk to anyone without him being present or without his permission. I started to think about how my life had did an entire 180 change. I was used to not talking to people unless they talked to me, but this was ridiculous. I had lost myself in this cycle; I had made myself believe what we shared was love. He had given all the warning signs from day one. In that first conversation we shared, he said, "Either you do what the fuck I say or get the fuck from around me." That statement right there was a huge red flag that screamed "controlling." I heard it, and I ignored it at the same time. I laughed at it like it was a joke, but he was serious. He meant exactly what he said because he showed it. Every time he told me to do something, and I didn't do it, we argued and eventually fought. Walking away would have been the normal thing to do, but who does the norm these days, right? I loved him, and he told me he loved me, too, and that it would never happen again. But the funny thing is that he told me that every time it happened. He used to cry with me as he was apologizing. He held me so tightly as he explained how it was my fault that this happened. Then he always said it was my mouth that got me fucked up every time. So, I tried to keep my mouth closed when he began to argue, but then he would fuss about me being childish for not saying anything. This was a problem that made him angrier. But when I argued back, he would complain that I was being disrespectful, which also made him angrier. So basically, it was a no-win situation. He just always had to be in control, or at least that is how I feel about it. It had become a norm for me. He was my best friend, my lover, my confidant, my sons' father, basically at this point, he was my everything.

And in 2016, he became my husband. After everything, people were upset with me, but this was what we wanted. Looking back, I realized it was a mistake since things only got worse because he felt like he owned me then. I spent ten years of my life with his man. I learned a lot from him, through him, and about him. He was one of my greatest teachers in life. He has made me a better woman, mother, sister, friend, and advocate. Because of him, I now know my worth, my strengths and, more importantly, my purpose. Through experience, love, and abuse, I know that the life I once questioned and attempted to end is so much more precious now. I am not saying that this was easy. What I am saying is that everyone has had their trials and tribulations. Everyone falls or fails at some point in their life, but how you recover is your testimony. Please don't stay down and wallow in distress. Get back up and stride like it never happened, remembering every step of the way that made you who you are, and keep striving for success on your way up.

Crazy thing is that some people feel he doesn't love if he doesn't beat. Being in an abusive relationship is hard. It's embarrassing, sometimes even confusing. It's a job, but it's also rewarding if you make it out alive. All I am saying is that there are warning signs, and you should be very aware of them. I wasn't then, but I am fully aware now. As a matter of fact, I have even been known to second-guess myself a time or two. I convinced myself to never love again, but thank God for prayer and forgiveness. I am so prepared to run the other way.

I Am My Sister's Keeper

Here are some of the warning signs that you should be aware of if you believe you are in a relationship with an abusive man—he:

- has to be in control at all times;
- is jealous or possessive;
- isolates you from the world;
- has a violent temper and quickly changes moods;
- monitors your whereabouts, activities, and spending;
- pressures you to move fast into a relationship/commitment;
- has been in an abusive relationship before;
- believes in stereotypical gender roles;
- experiences most emotions in the form of anger and has difficulty expressing other emotions;
- does not listen to you when you say no or try to assert your boundaries;
- is cruel to children and insensitive to their suffering; and
- has multiple personalities.

Please know that you are not alone, it is not your fault, and you do not have to stay there.

I Am My Sister's Keeper

Nydia Shatanya Wells-Evans, a New Orleans native, is a survivor of as well as an advocate and public speaker for domestic violence. Nydia uses her voice and experiences to let people know that they are not alone and help is available. Nydia has a passion for helping others. She also has a desire to empower, uplift, and encourage those around her. She encourages everyone to speak up and out because the life you save may be your very own. Nydia has been campaigning against domestic violence for several years and maintains a passion to spread the word about domestic violence awareness.

The Strength Is in Your Sisterly Bond

Tywauna
Wilson

"They did all they could do. She didn't make it." I will never forget hearing those words after the unexpected passing of my best friend. How could it be? It had to be some mistake. I pride myself on being my sister's keeper, yet I couldn't keep my sister this time. Why did she have to go at that moment? Even though I still needed her here, I believe her parents had been waiting long enough and needed her more. Being called to be your sister's keeper is a bond created by God. Many people will not understand it because the blessings of being your sister's keeper surpasses all human understanding. In this case, our bond extended 21 years of good times, difficult moments, and memories to last a lifetime. She was more than a friend; she was my sister. She kept me laughing. She kept me thinking and dreaming outside of my box. She kept me at peace. There is nothing like the love of a sister, the wisdom shared between sisters, and the faith to get through each day that comes with having sisterly relationships.

The world tries to display images of women at odds, tearing each other down, and being unkind and untrustworthy to one another. Oftentimes, the media tries to devalue the richness and necessity that having sister friends in your life brings. Your role in being your sister's keeper is simple. You are charged with the responsibility to (1) Encourage, (2) Support, and (3) Provide Accountability to your fellow sisters.

A Sister Is There to Encourage

"When you encourage others, you in the process are encouraged because you're making a commitment and difference in that person's life. Encouragement really does make a difference." -
Zig Ziglar

In the craziness of today's changing times, who doesn't need encouragement? It is easy to get side tracked and caught up in the trenches of life that you can feel like you are all alone. I can remember when I was getting ready to take my medical laboratory science certification test to be able to work in my industry. Passing that test was necessary for me to be able to work in my field. I took the test the first time and failed. I was down. I couldn't shake it. I was talking to one of my sister friends from high school about my dilemma. She gave me valuable tips and words of encouragement to prepare me to take the test again. I paid the fee and took the test again. Round two! The result was the same. I failed. At this point, I was defeated. My job was in jeopardy. I was ashamed. Why couldn't I pass the test? My friend took the time to help me study as I prepared to take it a third time. She would send me encouraging prayers and text messages telling me "You got this" and "You were meant to be a scientist" and other encouraging messages. When you are blessed to have an amazing sisterhood circle, they will step in for you when you are too weak and frustrated to keep moving. They will carry the baton for you until you are ready to pick it back up. She was right. I could do it, and the third time was the charm. The rest is history! I have been a scientist for over fifteen years and counting.

A Sister Is There to Support

*She is clothed with strength and dignity, and she laughs without
fear of the future. When she speaks, her words are wise, and
she gives instructions with kindness. —Proverbs 31:25-26*

Your sister is there to support you during your time
of need. She is there to take an active role in your tribe
and bring things to your attention even before they
become a big deal or a problem. She also looks for
ways to push you to the next level. Early on in my
business, I had a sorority sister who recommended me
for my first corporate event. She knew I was in the
beginning stages of getting my business off the ground
when she leveraged her business connections so that I
could have an opportunity to showcase my expertise
and get paid while doing it. She didn't have to do this
for me. She didn't owe me anything. It was just the help
that I needed to get my business going in a positive
direction. Support can come in the form of leveraging
a connection; it could be financial assistance, spiritual
covering, physical support, etc. Whatever it is that you
need, be it in your personal or professional life, we all
need our sisters to help us move from surviving to
thriving. You have to be open and flexible to receive.
Remember, a closed fist can never receive a blessing.

A Sister Is There to Provide Accountability

God is within her, she will not fall. -Psalm 46:5

Have you ever set goals, but you didn't tell your sister what they were? Maybe you didn't tell her because you were not confident in your ability to make them a reality. Or maybe you were not sure if you could trust your sister with your goals in the event that you couldn't meet them. Well, truth is, having someone keep you accountable to your goals can be scary at first, but it is necessary for your success and well-being. When I was working on my first book collaboration, in which I was taking on the Visionary Author role, I wanted to delay the project and start on it at some time in the distant future, date to be determined. I was eight months pregnant with my daughter, and I knew my life was getting real. Valid point, right? I started to make excuses of all the reasons that this was not a right time or why I didn't have the time to work on this book project. My sister friend pushed me to stay accountable to the goal of starting and finishing my book before the end of the year was out. It was a goal that I had set earlier in the year with no real timeline. She assured me we could get it done. We set an aggressive schedule for getting authors on board, writing, marketing, and getting this book out to the public. We DID IT! It was a season of birth. I gave birth to my daughter and to my book all within four months of each other. It definitely took faith and hard work that everything would come to fruition. I am thankful to my sister for holding me accountable to get the project done. Had it not been for me sharing my book goal with her and her seeing the value it would bring to the world, my book would still be an idea.

My Sister's Keeper to the End

May the Lord give strength to his people! May the Lord bless his people with peace! -Psalm 29:11

As you can see, it is important for you to be your sister's keeper as well as your sister to be your keeper. When I started this chapter, I talked about one of my favorite sisters. Her name was Alicia. She had a significant part in my life. We met in college and stayed friends until she danced up out of this life at the tender age of 39 on February 14, 2020. I use the word danced because she was always dancing and smiling. We shared a lot of milestones including college graduation, numerous birthdays, various celebrations, and she was in my wedding and there for the dedication of my daughter. A lot of people knew her, talked highly of her, and were genuinely just glad they had the chance to know her. Although life presented its own unique challenges to her, she made lemonade out of her lemons for the time she did have on this earth. It was an honor to be asked by her family to speak at my sister's funeral and talk about her, us, and the blessing of experiencing that type of sisterly bond in my life. Even to the end, I realize, I never stopped being my sister's keeper. I kept holding her hand and walking with her until her mom said, *I will take your sister's hand from here.* I felt her saying, *you had her all these years, and now WE got you!*

When life gets tough, you have your sister. When life is amazing, you have your sister. When you don't have the energy to even think, you have your sister. Through it all, you have your sister. Don't forget, it is your responsibility to encourage, support, and provide accountability to your fellow sisters for as long as you are blessed to do so just as they have done for you. Nothing replaces the bonds you will form with your sisters. Be blessed, Sis, and don't forget, you are your sister's keeper!

Tywauna Wilson is a best-selling author, entrepreneur, medical laboratory scientist, and an award-winning leadership maven. She is the founder and CEO of Trendy Elite Coaching and Consulting. She is the author of *Some Leaders Wear Lab Coats*, the visionary author of the *Leadership Tidbits* book series, and host of the *Leadership Tidbits with Coach Tee Wilson* and *eLABorate Topics* podcasts online at Direct Impact Broadcasting. Tywauna has over 15 years of diverse laboratory leadership experience. Her mission is to empower and train one million leaders worldwide to be able to utilize their skills to lead with confidence and leave a career legacy that makes them proud.

Learn more about Tywauna at LinkedIn (Tywauna Wilson) and her website (www.coachteewilson.com).

Check Out Our Other Anthologies!

Christian-Friendly Drama by Publisher Telishia Berry

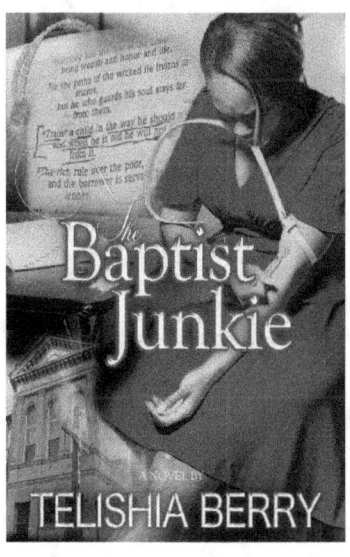